Betty Crocker
quick
&easy
cookbook

30 minutes or less to dinner

BICENTENNIAL
1807
WILEY
2007
BICENTENNIAL

Wiley Publishing, Inc.

Copyright © 2007 by General Mills, Minneapolis, MN. All rights reserved.

Published by Wiley Publishing, Inc., Hoboken, NJ

No part of this publication may be reproduced, stored in a retrieval system, or transmitted in any form or by any means, electronic, mechanical, photocopying, recording, scanning, or otherwise, except as permitted under Section 107 or 108 of the 1976 United States Copyright Act, without either the prior written permission of the Publisher, or authorization through payment of the appropriate per-copy fee to the Copyright Clearance Center, Inc., 222 Rosewood Drive, Danvers, MA 01923, (978) 750-8400, fax (978) 750-4470, or on the web at www.copyright.com. Requests to the Publisher for permission should be addressed to the Permissions Department, John Wiley & Sons, Inc., 111 River Street, Hoboken, NJ 07030, (201) 748-6011, fax (201) 748-6008, or online at http://www.wiley.com/go/permissions.

Trademarks: Wiley and the Wiley Publishing logo are trademarks or registered trademarks of John Wiley & Sons and/or its affiliates. All other trademarks referred to herein are trademarks of General Mills. Wiley Publishing, Inc., is not associated with any product or vendor mentioned in this book.

Limit of Liability/Disclaimer of Warranty: While the publisher and author have used their best efforts in preparing this book, they make no representations or warranties with respect to the accuracy or completeness of the contents of this book and specifically disclaim any implied warranties of merchantability or fitness for a particular purpose. No warranty may be created or extended by sales representatives or written sales materials. The advice and strategies contained herein may not be suitable for your situation. You should consult with a professional where appropriate. Neither the publisher nor author shall be liable for any loss of profit or any other commercial damages, including but not limited to special, incidental, consequential, or other damages.

For general information on our other products and services or for technical support, please contact our Customer Care Department within the United States at (800) 762-2974, outside the United States at (317) 572-3993 or fax (317) 572-4002.

Wiley also publishes its books in a variety of electronic formats. Some content that appears in print may not be available in electronic books. For more information about Wiley products, visit our web site at www.wiley.com.

Library of Congress Cataloging-in-Publication Data:

Crocker, Betty.

Betty Crocker quick & easy cookbook / Betty Crocker.—2nd ed.

p. cm.

Rev. ed. of: Betty Crocker's quick & easy cookbook. 2003.

Includes index.

ISBN: 978-0-470-14459-6 (custom edition)

1. Quick and easy cookery. 2. Dinners and dining. I. Crocker, Betty. Betty Crocker's quick & easy cookbook. II. Title. III. Title: Betty Crocker quick and easy cookbook. IV. Title: Quick & easy cookbook.

TX833.5.C68524 2007

641.5'55—dc22

2006014215

Manufactured in China

10 9 8 7 6 5 4 3 2 1

Second Edition

Cover photo: Country Eggs in Tortilla Cups (page 244)

GENERAL MILLS

Director, Book and Online Publishing: Kim Walter

Manager, Cookbook Publishing: Lois Tlusty

Editor: Lori Fox

Recipe Development and Testing: Betty Crocker Kitchens

Photography and Food Styling: General Mills Photography Studios

WILEY PUBLISHING, INC.

Publisher: Natalie Chapman

Executive Editor: Anne Ficklen

Editor: Adam Kowit

Production Editor: Leslie Anglin

Cover Design: Paul Dinovo

Interior Design and Layout: Holly Wittenberg

Photography Art Direction: Sue Schultz

Manufacturing Manager: Kevin Watt

The Betty Crocker Kitchens seal guarantees success in your kitchen. Every recipe has been tested in America's Most Trusted Kitchens™ to meet our high standards of reliability, easy preparation and great taste.

FIND MORE GREAT IDEAS AT

BettyCrocker.com

Dear Friends,

It's almost dinner time—how did the day go by so fast? It's tempting to just go with a bowl of cereal or order pizza, but doesn't a home-cooked dinner sound a lot better?

Consider this book your roadmap to dinner by the shortest route possible. Every recipe takes 30 minutes or less from start to finish. (Try getting to the drive-through window and back that quickly!)

There are fun meals like Quick Chicken Quesadillas and delectable treats like Grilled Salmon with Nectarine Salsa, plus pizza, sandwiches, breakfast for dinner—and even some super-streamlined soups. Who knew you could make chicken noodle soup with fresh veggies in only 30 minutes?

Time is something we could all use a second helping of, but most days we're lucky to steal a few free morsels at best. So on days when every minute counts, let *Betty Crocker Quick & Easy Cookbook* put you in the fast lane to dinner, so you can spend your precious free moments with the family, or anyone.

Warmly,

Betty Crocker

contents

"24/7": great tips
for quick cooking

What a busy week it's been! Priorities likely include simplifying life by making dinners more quickly. It's easy enough to phone in a pizza order, get fast food or open a can of soup, but let's face it, having a homemade meal is more satisfying! Once you know the easy tricks for quick cooking, you can make anything you want even faster! Browse all the fast-track tips below.

DO IT NOW, SAVE TIME LATER Taking a few more moments to get ingredients ready ahead really saves you time in the long run. On one of those hectic nights when every extra minute counts, you will be glad you did. Here are some of the best ideas:

- **Burgers:** Make extra hamburger patties or meatballs and freeze in resealable food-storage plastic freezer bag up to 4 months.

- **Ground beef:** Brown extra ground beef and freeze desired amounts in resealable food-storage plastic freezer bags up to 3 months.

- **Meat and Poultry:** Cut raw meat and poultry into strips or cubes; arrange in single layer on foil-lined cookie sheet and freeze until firm. Put desired amounts into resealable food-storage plastic freezer bags and freeze up to 9 months.

- **Cooked Chicken:** Cook extra chicken and cut it up. Put desired amounts in resealable food-storage plastic freezer bags and freeze up to 4 months.

- **Pasta and Rice:** Cook and drain extra pasta or rice. After draining, toss pasta or rice with a little olive oil or vegetable oil to keep it from sticking together. Put desired amounts in reseable food-storage plastic bags; refrigerate up to 5 days or freeze up to 6 months.

- **Veggies:** Chop, slice or dice fresh veggies like onions, bell peppers, carrots and celery. Arrange in single layer on foil-lined cookie sheet and freeze until firm. Put desired amounts in resealable food-storage plastic freezer bags and freeze up to 1 month.

THINNER IS FASTER To cook boneless skinless chicken breasts faster, pound them with a meat mallet or rolling pin between sheets of waxed paper or plastic wrap until they're about 1/4 inch thick.

NO CLEANUP Line cookie sheets and baking pans with nonstick or regular foil before baking breaded chicken strips, fish sticks, French fries or anything similar. When it's baked, remove the food and toss the foil.

A SPEEDIER MASH To slash the cooking time for homemade mashed potatoes, cut the potatoes into 1- to 1 1/2-inch pieces. This works great for other veggies, too!

BOIL WATER FASTER To jump-start boiling water, start with hot water and cover the saucepan with a lid.

NO MORE STICKY SITUATIONS When measuring syrup, honey or other sticky stuff, spray measuring spoons and cups with cooking spray first—it'll slide right out!

QUICKER PASTA TOSS If you frequently toss pasta with veggies, don't cook those veggies separately; just add frozen or fresh veggies to the pasta cooking water during the last few minutes of cooking, and drain the whole works together!

Betty Crocker quick & easy cookbook

gizmos, gadgets
and other great stuff

It's so true, having the right tool or gadget can shave off minutes when time really matters. We don't have room to list all the great little items available, but look for these handy kitchen helpers in department or discount stores, kitchenware stores, over the Internet or even in large supermarkets or hardware stores.

Chopper: Nonelectric choppers are great for handling small amounts of ingredients like onions, bell peppers, olives or other lightweight foods. The food goes into a glass or plastic hopper and a set of cutting blades does the work when you either press a plunger up and down or turn a handle. Or, by all means, use an electric mini-food processor.

Cutting wheel (rolling mincer): A cool little handheld tool with two cutting blades that you roll back and forth over fresh herbs, garlic or small green onions on a cutting board to finely chop or mince.

Flexible cutting mat: Almost paper thin, these tough, flexible mats let you easily transfer ingredients from the mat to another container by folding the mat in half over the container and letting the ingredients fall in.

Kitchen scissors: Look for heavy-duty all-purpose kitchen scissors. Cut up fresh herbs, dried fruit, canned whole tomatoes and marshmallows; cut tortillas into strips or pita breads in half. A specific type of scissors called poultry scissors is designed to cut through chicken bones and thinner, lighter turkey bones (great to use if you economize by cutting up whole chickens into quarters or to cut the tips of chicken wings for zesty buffalo wings).

Nonstick anything: Nonstick surfaces mean a lot less cleanup, especially when it comes to skillets! Just make sure always to use silicone or plastic utensils so the surface won't get scratched. Over time, all those scratches remove the coating and reduce the nonstick qualities.

Pasta server (pasta fork/spoon): If your cooked pasta keeps slip-sliding away, get one of those dandy pasta servers! In one swoop, you can gather up pasta, and it works especially well for long pasta.

Pour-off sieve: A crescent-shaped straining device that fits over the rim of a variety of pot and pan sizes. All you do is tilt and pour off the liquid. If you usually toss your pasta with a sauce, this tool with its one-step process saves you from washing a colander!

Spring-loaded scoop: This multipurpose tool comes in various sizes for scooping ice cream, batters and doughs for baked goods, meatballs and melon balls. The nifty wire scraper inside these scoops neatly releases whatever is inside when the handle lever is pressed.

Whisk: Available in metal and silicone versions, this kitchen staple saves time as it blends and whips egg mixtures, sauces and lightweight batters. A good-quality wire whisk is made from a heavier-gauge metal, and has more wires and a solid metal handle, often about 1 inch in diameter. This type of whisk can hold up to denser, heavier mixtures better than inexpensive, lightweight or silicone models. In nonstick cookware, use only silicone whisks so they don't scratch. Stock multiple whisks in a variety of sizes so just the right one is always available and not in the dishwasher!

the quick cook's pantry
for the 5:30 challenge

What's for dinner? Most of us start thinking about what's for dinner about an hour or two before we actually sit down to eat. Whether you're still at work or the kids are just getting off the bus, that's not very far ahead of time. A well-stocked pantry is a solution for this last-minute scramble and is a terrific meal-planning tool. Since we all like different foods and have different needs, no one pantry list works for everyone, but this list of quick picks provides the ingredients for a great start!

VEGETABLES

- Prewashed and precut fresh vegetables
- Frozen veggies (plain or blends)
- Salad kits
- Canned veggies (mushrooms, corn)
- Ready-to-heat-and-eat refrigerated potato side dishes
- Frozen and refrigerated ready-to-cook potatoes
- Boxed instant potato mixes

FRUITS

- Prewashed and precut fresh fruit
- Frozen fruit
- Jarred and canned fruit

MEAT, POULTRY, FISH AND SEAFOOD

- Ground beef and turkey
- Precut meats and chicken
- Boneless skinless chicken breasts
- Thinly cut meats and poultry
- Steaks and chops instead of roasts
- Heat-and-eat seasoned roasts
- Rotisserie chicken
- Refrigerated shredded barbecued meat and poultry
- Deli products
- Canned and vacuum-packed pouch products
- Refrigerated seasoned meat and poultry strips
- Precooked sausage links and rings
- Frozen meatballs
- Frozen breaded chicken and fish
- Frozen peeled deveined shrimp or breaded shrimp

DAIRY CASE

- Milk
- Eggs or fat-free egg product
- Butter or margarine
- Shredded, sliced, crumbled and cubed cheeses
- Cheese spreads, cheese loaves
- Grated Parmesan cheese
- Cream cheese
- Half-and-half, whipping cream
- Sour cream

NONPERISHABLE STAPLES

- Soups and chili
- Pasta and pizza sauces
- Jarred gravy
- Gravy and sauce mixes
- Canned seasoned tomato products
- Canned chicken and beef broth
- Canned beans (plain, refried or baked beans)
- Dried fruits
- Nuts
- Vegetable oil
- Olive oil
- Cooking spray

PASTAS AND GRAINS

- Fresh refrigerated pasta (plain or filled)
- Frozen egg noodles
- Frozen ravioli or gnocchi
- Angel hair or vermicelli pasta
- Couscous (plain or flavored)
- Flavored pasta and noodle mixes
- Instant white or brown rice
- Flavored rice mixes

CONDIMENTS

- Salsa
- Ketchup
- Barbecue sauce
- Mustard (yellow, Dijon, honey-mustard)
- Mayonnaise or salad dressing
- Soy sauce, teriyaki sauce
- Marinades
- Worcestershire sauce
- Balsamic vinegar
- Salad dressings
- Pickles/olives
- Dried herbs (basil, oregano, Italian seasoning, marjoram, thyme)
- Spices (cinnamon, ginger, cloves, pumpkin pie spice, chili powder, cumin)
- Seasonings and seasoning mixes (garlic powder and salt, lemon-pepper, Cajun, barbecue)
- Honey
- Maple syrup
- Jams, jellies, marmalades, preserves
- Jarred chopped garlic
- Refrigerated or jarred pesto
- Bouillon granules or cubes

BREAD AND BAKING MIX

- Tortillas
- Prebaked Italian pizza crusts
- Taco shells
- Bread crumbs (plain or seasoned)
- Croutons
- Stuffing mix or cubes
- Frozen dinner rolls
- Refrigerated dough products (biscuits, rolls, pizza dough, pie crust)
- French bread
- Pita breads
- English muffins
- Bread (your favorite type of loaf)
- Bisquick mix (for pancakes, biscuits, dumplings)

ULTRA-CONVENIENCE

- Frozen pizza
- Frozen meal starter kits
- Frozen seasoned pasta blends
- Boxed meal kits
- Stop by the deli
- Pick up your favorite takeout
- Order pizza
- Make reservations

1 lightbites

Instant Appetizers

Have you ever had an appetizer emergency and thought the only thing you could come up with was a bag of chips with dip or salsa? Well, the ideas here are a little more exciting than that!

1 **Warmed Olives and Roasted Almonds with Lemon-Olive Oil Drizzle:** Heat oven to 350°F. In a shallow baking dish, mix equal amounts of your favorite mixture of olives (drained) and lightly salted roasted whole almonds. Drizzle lightly with extra-virgin olive oil, sprinkle with grated lemon peel and toss. Heat briefly just to warm olives. Serve with sliced crusty bread or crackers.

2 **Basil-Mascarpone Spread:** Ont o a shallow serving dish, spread about 8 ounces of mascarpone cheese or softened cream cheese; spoon basil pesto over the top and sprinkle with chopped red bell pepper. Serve with baguette slices or crackers.

3 **Parmesan and Dates:** Cut a piece of Parmesan or Asiago cheese into cube-size chunks (they won't be nice and even, but that's okay). Top with the same size piece of dried date or fig; secure with a toothpick. Serve with baguette slices or crackers.

4 **Blue Cheese Waffle Fries:** Heat frozen waffle fries or cottage fries in oven as directed on the package. About 2 to 5 minutes before they're done, remove them from the oven and sprinkle with crumbled blue or Gorgonzola cheese. Continue baking just until the cheese begins to melt. Have a bottle of Buffalo wings hot sauce available for those who like things spicy!

5 **Italian Snack Mix:** Drizzle popcorn, mini bagel chips, mini pretzels and Parmesan- or pizza-flavored fish-shaped crackers with melted butter. Sprinkle with garlic powder, onion powder, dried basil leaves and dried oregano leaves; toss gently.

6 **So-Simple Salsa Dip:** Mix equal parts of salsa and softened cream cheese, adding milk if needed. Serve with tortilla chips.

7 **Yogonanas:** Poke end of wooden stick into banana half; roll banana in your favorite flavor of yogurt, then roll in crushed cereal, granola or cookies.

8 **That Marshmallow Creme Fruit Dip:** In a medium bowl, beat an 8-ounce package of softened cream cheese, a 7-ounce jar of marshmallow creme and 1 tablespoon of milk or cream with an electric mixer until smooth and creamy. Serve with fresh fruit, cookies or graham crackers as dippers.

9 **Pepperoni Pizza Nachos:** Heat oven to 400°F. On a foil-lined cookie sheet, arrange tortilla chips. Top with sliced pepperoni, pizza sauce and shredded mozzarella or pizza cheese blend. Bake 4 to 6 minutes or until hot and cheese is melted.

10 **Graham Cracker Nachos:** On a serving plate, arrange graham crackers. Drizzle melted peanut butter or almond butter over crackers; top as desired with ingredients like mini marshmallows, mini candies, sliced fresh fruit, dried fruit, cereal or trail mix.

This icon means: ◔ 20 minutes or less

Quick Chicken Quesadillas

1 package (6 oz) refrigerated cooked Southwest-flavor chicken breast strips*

1/2 cup chunky-style salsa

8 flour tortillas (6 to 8 inch)

Cooking spray

2 cups finely shredded Colby–Monterey Jack cheese blend (8 oz)

1/4 cup sour cream

1 Cut chicken into bite-size pieces. In small bowl, mix chicken and salsa.

2 Spray 1 side of 1 tortilla with cooking spray; place sprayed side down in 10-inch skillet. Layer with 1/4 of the chicken mixture and 1/2 cup of the cheese. Top with another tortilla; spray top of tortilla with cooking spray.

3 Cook uncovered over medium heat 4 to 6 minutes, carefully turning after 2 minutes, until golden brown and cheese is melted. Repeat with remaining tortillas, chicken mixture and cheese. To serve, cut quesadillas into wedges. Serve with sour cream and, if desired, additional salsa.

4 servings (1 quesadilla each)

Can't find the refrigerated seasoned chicken? Substitute 1 1/2 cups chopped rotisserie or other cooked chicken.

Instant **Success!**

If you like veggies, try Quick Chicken-Vegetable Quesadillas. Just sprinkle 2 tablespoons chopped tomato, 1 tablespoon sliced ripe olives and 1 tablespoon sliced green onions over the cheese for each quesadilla.

1 Serving: Calories 480 (Calories from Fat 250); Total Fat 28g (Saturated Fat 15g; Trans Fat 1g); Cholesterol 95mg; Sodium 920mg; Total Carbohydrate 30g (Dietary Fiber 2g; Sugars 3g); Protein 28g ✎ **% Daily Value:** Vitamin A 15%; Vitamin C 4%; Calcium 50%; Iron 15% ✎ **Exchanges:** 2 Starch, 3 Lean Meat, 3 1/2 Fat ✎ **Carbohydrate Choices:** 2

Veggie Quesadillas

Prep Time **15 Minutes**
Start to Finish **20 Minutes**

1 cup shredded zucchini

1 small tomato, seeded, chopped
(1/2 cup)

1 tablespoon chopped fresh or 1 teaspoon
dried oregano leaves

1/2 teaspoon garlic-pepper blend

8 whole wheat flour tortillas (8 inch)

2 cups shredded Italian cheese blend
(8 oz)

Tomato pasta sauce or marinara sauce,
heated, if desired

1 Heat oven to 350°F. In medium bowl, mix zucchini, tomato, oregano and
garlic-pepper blend.

2 On ungreased large cookie sheet, place 4 tortillas. Sprinkle 1/2 cup of the
cheese evenly over each of the 4 tortillas. Spoon 1/4 of the vegetable mixture
over cheese. Top with remaining tortillas.

3 Bake about 6 minutes or until hot and cheese is melted. Cut each
quesadilla into wedges. Serve with pasta sauce.

4 servings (1 quesadilla each)

Make it a Meal

*Ramp up supper by adding a
bagged salad mix and dressing.*

1 Serving: Calories 300 (Calories from Fat 150); Total Fat 16g (Saturated Fat 10g; Trans Fat 0.5g); Cholesterol 40mg;
Sodium 680mg; Total Carbohydrate 20g (Dietary Fiber 4g; Sugars 2g); Protein 18g ✂ **% Daily Value:** Vitamin A 15%;
Vitamin C 6%; Calcium 45%; Iron 8% ✂ **Exchanges:** 1 1/2 Starch, 2 Medium-Fat Meat, 1/2 Fat ✂ **Carbohydrate
Choices:** 1

Super Chicken Nachos

6 oz tortilla chips (6 cups)

1/2 cup chopped ripe avocado

1/2 teaspoon ground cumin

1 large tomato, seeded, chopped
(1 cup)

1 cup shredded rotisserie or other cooked
chicken

1 cup shredded Monterey Jack cheese
(4 oz)

Salsa and sour cream, if desired

1 Heat oven to 400°F. Line cookie sheet with foil. Place tortilla chips
on cookie sheet.

2 In small bowl, mix avocado, cumin and tomato; spoon over chips.
Top with chicken and cheese.

3 Bake 3 to 5 minutes or until cheese is melted. Serve with salsa and
sour cream.

6 servings

Easy Add-On

*Everybody likes dips for
dunking, so add purchased bean
dip or salsa con queso on the
side. For bigger appetites, add
fresh fruit or salads from the deli.*

1 Serving: Calories 280 (Calories from Fat 150); Total Fat 16g (Saturated Fat 5g; Trans Fat 0g); Cholesterol 35mg;
Sodium 390mg; Total Carbohydrate 20g (Dietary Fiber 2g; Sugars 1g); Protein 14g ~ **% Daily Value:** Vitamin A 10%;
Vitamin C 4%; Calcium 15%; Iron 10% ~ **Exchanges:** 1 1/2 Starch, 1 1/2 Lean Meat, 2 Fat ~ **Carbohydrate
Choices:** 1

Buffalo-Style Chicken Nuggets

1 1/2 cups Corn Chex® cereal

1/2 cup Original Bisquick® mix

2 teaspoons paprika

1/4 teaspoon seasoned salt

1/4 teaspoon ground red pepper
   (cayenne)

1 tablespoon vegetable oil

1 teaspoon red pepper sauce

1 lb boneless skinless chicken breasts,
   cut into 2-inch pieces

1/4 cup ranch dressing

1 Heat oven to 425°F. In 1-gallon resealable food-storage plastic bag, crush cereal with rolling pin. Add Bisquick mix, paprika, seasoned salt and ground red pepper to cereal; mix well.

2 In small bowl, mix oil and red pepper sauce. Coat chicken pieces with oil mixture.

3 Shake about 6 chicken pieces at a time in bag of cereal mixture until coated. Shake off any extra mixture. On ungreased cookie sheet, place chicken pieces in single layer.

4 Bake about 10 minutes or until chicken is no longer pink in center. Serve chicken with dressing.

4 servings

Easy Add-On

Add a side of crunchy dippers such as celery and carrot sticks to serve with these spicy nuggets. Any of your favorite sauces or salad dressings can be used for dipping.

1 Serving: Calories 340 (Calories from Fat 150); Total Fat 17g (Saturated Fat 3g; Trans Fat 0g); Cholesterol 75mg; Sodium 590mg; Total Carbohydrate 20g (Dietary Fiber 1g; Sugars 3g); Protein 27g ❧ **% Daily Value:** Vitamin A 20%; Vitamin C 4%; Calcium 8%; Iron 30% ❧ **Exchanges:** 1 1/2 Starch, 3 Very Lean Meat, 3 Fat ❧ **Carbohydrate Choices:** 1

Prep Time **10 Minutes**

Start to Finish **30 Minutes**

Chewy Pizza Bread

1 1/2 cups all-purpose flour

1 1/2 teaspoons baking powder

1/2 teaspoon salt

3/4 cup regular or nonalcoholic beer

1/2 cup tomato pasta sauce

1/3 cup shredded mozzarella cheese (1.5 oz)

Chopped fresh basil leaves, if desired

1 Heat oven to 425°F. Spray 8-inch square pan with cooking spray.

2 In medium bowl, mix flour, baking powder and salt. Stir in beer just until flour is moistened. Spread dough in pan. Spread pasta sauce over dough. Sprinkle with cheese.

3 Bake 15 to 20 minutes or until toothpick inserted in center comes out clean. Sprinkle with basil. Cut into 2-inch squares. Serve warm.

4 servings (4 squares each)

Easy Add-On

Pepperoni? Yes, go ahead and add slices of pepperoni on the sauce before topping with cheese.

1 Serving: Calories 230 (Calories from Fat 30); Total Fat 3.5g (Saturated Fat 1.5g; Trans Fat 0g); Cholesterol 5mg; Sodium 680mg; Total Carbohydrate 43g (Dietary Fiber 2g; Sugars 3g); Protein 8g ⁓ **% Daily Value:** Vitamin A 4%; Vitamin C 2%; Calcium 20%; Iron 15% ⁓ **Exchanges:** 3 Starch ⁓ **Carbohydrate Choices:** 3

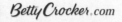

String Cheese Sticks with Dipping Sauce

2 1/4 cups Original Bisquick mix

2/3 cup milk

1 package (8 oz) plain or smoked
    string cheese

1 can (8 oz) pizza sauce

1 tablespoon butter or margarine, melted

1/4 teaspoon garlic powder

1 Heat oven to 450°F. In medium bowl, stir Bisquick mix and milk until soft dough forms; beat 30 seconds with spoon. Place dough on surface sprinkled with Bisquick mix; gently roll in Bisquick mix to coat. Shape into a ball; knead 10 times.

2 Roll dough into 12 × 8-inch rectangle, 1/4 inch thick. Cut into 8 (6 × 2-inch) rectangles. Roll each rectangle around 1 piece of cheese. Pinch edge into roll to seal; seal ends. Roll on surface to completely enclose cheese sticks. On ungreased cookie sheet, place sticks seam sides down.

3 Bake 8 to 10 minutes or until golden brown. Meanwhile, in 1-quart saucepan, heat pizza sauce over low heat until warm. In small bowl, mix butter and garlic powder; brush over warm cheese sticks before removing from cookie sheet. Serve warm with pizza sauce for dipping.

4 servings (2 cheese sticks each)

Speed it Up

If you don't have pizza sauce on hand, heat up your favorite pasta sauce instead.

1 Serving: Calories 500 (Calories from Fat 220); Total Fat 24g (Saturated Fat 12g; Trans Fat 2g); Cholesterol 40mg; Sodium 1540mg; Total Carbohydrate 50g (Dietary Fiber 2g; Sugars 10g); Protein 22g ✺ **% Daily Value:** Vitamin A 10%; Vitamin C 2%; Calcium 60%; Iron 20% ✺ **Exchanges:** 2 1/2 Starch, 1 Other Carbohydrate, 2 High-Fat Meat, 1 Fat ✺ **Carbohydrate Choices:** 3

light **bites**

Prep Time **20 Minutes**
Start to Finish **20 Minutes**

Tiny Meat and Cheese Bites

1 cup Giardiniera vegetable mix (from 16-oz jar), drained

40 cubes (1/2 inch) hard salami (about 1/2 lb)

40 cubes (1/2 inch) Swiss cheese (about 4 oz)

1 Cut larger vegetables into 1/2-inch pieces.

2 On each of 40 toothpicks, alternate pieces of salami, vegetables and cheese.

8 servings (5 skewers each)

Instant
Success!

Giardiniera is a mixture of pickled vegetables, such as carrots, cauliflower, red pepper and celery. You can usually find it in the supermarket with the pickles and olives.

1 Serving: Calories 170 (Calories from Fat 120); Total Fat 14g (Saturated Fat 6g; Trans Fat 0g); Cholesterol 35mg; Sodium 800mg; Total Carbohydrate 2g (Dietary Fiber 0g; Sugars 1g); Protein 10g ✥ **% Daily Value:** Vitamin A 4%; Vitamin C 0%; Calcium 10%; Iron 4% ✥ **Exchanges:** 1 1/2 High-Fat Meat ✥ **Carbohydrate Choices:** 0

Betty Crocker quick & easy cookbook

Mini Salmon Wraps

Prep Time **20 Minutes**
Start to Finish **30 Minutes**

2 packages (3 oz each) cream cheese, softened

2 tablespoons horseradish sauce

6 spinach, tomato or plain flour tortillas (8 to 10 inch)

1 medium cucumber, peeled, finely chopped (1 cup)

1/4 cup sour cream

1/4 cup chopped fresh dill weed

1/4 cup finely chopped red or yellow onion

8 oz salmon lox, cut into thin strips

1 In small bowl, mix cream cheese and horseradish sauce. Spread cream cheese mixture evenly over tortillas.

2 In small bowl, mix cucumber, sour cream, dill weed and onion; spread over cream cheese mixture. Arrange salmon strips over cucumber mixture. Roll up tortillas tightly.

3 Cover and refrigerate wraps 10 minutes or until ready to serve. If desired, cut each wrap into 8 pieces.

6 servings (8 pieces each)

Speed it Up

Beat the clock! Make these sophisticated wraps up to 24 hours ahead; cover with plastic wrap and refrigerate.

1 Serving: Calories 310 (Calories from Fat 150); Total Fat 17g (Saturated Fat 8g; Trans Fat 1g); Cholesterol 45mg; Sodium 610mg; Total Carbohydrate 27g (Dietary Fiber 1g; Sugars 2g); Protein 13g ✵ **% Daily Value:** Vitamin A 10%; Vitamin C 4%; Calcium 10%; Iron 10% ✵ **Exchanges:** 2 Starch, 1 Very Lean Meat, 3 Fat ✵ **Carbohydrate Choices:** 2

Spicy Lemon Shrimp with Basil Mayonnaise

1 tablespoon grated lemon peel

3 tablespoons lemon juice

3/4 teaspoon crushed red pepper flakes

1/2 teaspoon salt

2 cloves garlic, finely chopped

2 tablespoons olive or vegetable oil

1 lb uncooked deveined peeled large shrimp (22 to 25 shrimp), thawed if frozen, tail shells removed

1/2 cup loosely packed fresh basil leaves

1/2 cup low-fat mayonnaise or salad dressing

1 Set oven control to broil. In medium glass or plastic bowl, mix lemon peel, lemon juice, red pepper flakes, salt, garlic and 1 tablespoon of the oil. Add shrimp; toss to coat. In ungreased 15 × 10 × 1-inch pan, spread shrimp.

2 Broil shrimp with tops 2 to 3 inches from heat 3 to 5 minutes or until shrimp are pink.

3 In food processor, place basil and remaining 1 tablespoon oil. Cover; process until chopped. Add mayonnaise. Cover; process until smooth. Serve shrimp with mayonnaise.

4 servings (6 shrimp and 2 tablespoons sauce each)

Instant **Success!**

Using frozen shrimp is super convenient, but pat the thawed shrimp dry before adding to the oil mixture. Reach dinnertime even faster by making and refrigerating the basil mayonnaise up to a day before.

1 Serving: Calories 250 (Calories from Fat 160); Total Fat 18g (Saturated Fat 2.5g; Trans Fat 0g); Cholesterol 170mg; Sodium 690mg; Total Carbohydrate 4g (Dietary Fiber 0g; Sugars 2g); Protein 18g ✏ **% Daily Value:** Vitamin A 15%; Vitamin C 6%; Calcium 4%; Iron 15% ✏ **Exchanges:** 2 1/2 Very Lean Meat, 3 1/2 Fat ✏ **Carbohydrate Choices:** 0

Grilled Veggies and Steak

1 package (6 oz) small fresh portabella
mushrooms

1/2 lb beef sirloin steak (about 3/4 inch
thick), cut into 3/4-inch cubes

1 cup frozen pearl onions (from 1-lb bag),
thawed

1/2 cup plus 2 tablespoons balsamic
vinaigrette

1/2 cup halved grape or cherry
tomatoes

1 Heat gas or charcoal grill. In large bowl, place mushrooms, beef, onions
and 1/2 cup of the vinaigrette; toss to coat. Let stand 10 minutes; drain. Place
mixture in grill basket (grill "wok"). Place basket on cookie sheet to carry to
grill to catch drips.

2 Place basket on grill. Cover grill; cook over medium-high heat 7 to 9 minutes, shaking basket or stirring beef mixture twice, until vegetables are tender
and beef is desired doneness. Stir in tomatoes.

3 Spoon beef mixture into serving dish. Stir in remaining 2 tablespoons
vinaigrette.

4 servings

Make it a Meal

*Throw in a ciabatta loaf or some
petits pains, and maybe a jar of
store-bought tapenade spread
for a light summertime dinner.*

1 Serving: Calories 150 (Calories from Fat 45); Total Fat 5g (Saturated Fat 1g; Trans Fat 0g); Cholesterol 30mg; Sodium
350mg; Total Carbohydrate 10g (Dietary Fiber 1g; Sugars 5g); Protein 15g ☙ **% Daily Value:** Vitamin A 4%; Vitamin C 6%;
Calcium 0%; Iron 8% ☙ **Exchanges:** 1 Vegetable, 2 Very Lean Meat, 1 Fat ☙ **Carbohydrate Choices:** 1/2

Prep Time **10 Minutes**

Start to Finish **30 Minutes**

Fresh Mozzarella and Tomato

4 medium tomatoes, cut into 1/4-inch slices

8 oz fresh mozzarella cheese, cut into 1/4-inch slices

2 tablespoons extra-virgin olive oil

2 tablespoons balsamic or red wine vinegar

2 tablespoons chopped fresh basil leaves

Freshly ground pepper

1 On round plate, arrange tomato and cheese slices alternately. Drizzle oil and vinegar over tomatoes and cheese. Sprinkle with basil and pepper.

2 Let stand at room temperature 20 minutes to blend flavors before serving. Cover and refrigerate leftovers.

4 servings

Instant **Success!**

Ripe tomatoes at their peak of flavor are essential to this simple but satisfying combination. Those mealy, weak-colored tomatoes just won't do, thank you. Serve with breadsticks and a nice medium- to light-bodied red wine.

1 Serving: Calories 260 (Calories from Fat 170); Total Fat 18g (Saturated Fat 8g; Trans Fat 0g); Cholesterol 30mg; Sodium 310mg; Total Carbohydrate 8g (Dietary Fiber 2g; Sugars 4g); Protein 16g ❧ **% Daily Value:** Vitamin A 30%; Vitamin C 25%; Calcium 45%; Iron 4% ❧ **Exchanges:** 1 Vegetable, 2 Medium-Fat Meat, 1 1/2 Fat ❧ **Carbohydrate Choices:** 1/2

Roast Beef Bruschetta

Prep Time **20 Minutes**
Start to Finish **30 Minutes**

1 loaf (1 lb) baguette French bread, cut into 30 (1/4-inch) slices

2 tablespoons olive or vegetable oil

5 small plum (Roma) tomatoes

1/2 cup chive-and-onion cream cheese spread (from 8-oz container)

1/2 lb thinly sliced cooked roast beef

1/4 teaspoon coarsely ground pepper

8 medium green onions, sliced (1/2 cup)

1 Heat oven to 375°F. Brush both sides of bread slices with oil. Place on ungreased cookie sheet. Bake about 5 minutes or until crisp. Cool 5 minutes.

2 Meanwhile, cut each tomato into 6 slices; set aside. Spread cream cheese over each bread slice. Top with beef; sprinkle with pepper. Top with tomato slices and onions.

6 servings (5 bruschetta each)

Speed it Up

It's great to be able to make some foods before you need them. Toast the bread slices a day ahead of time, and store loosely covered at room temperature. Top them up to 1 hour ahead, then cover and place in the fridge until serving.

1 Serving: Calories 400 (Calories from Fat 170); Total Fat 19g (Saturated Fat 7g; Trans Fat 1g); Cholesterol 45mg; Sodium 600mg; Total Carbohydrate 41g (Dietary Fiber 3g; Sugars 2g); Protein 18g ❧ **% Daily Value:** Vitamin A 10%; Vitamin C 10%; Calcium 8%; Iron 20% ❧ **Exchanges:** 2 1/2 Starch, 1 Vegetable, 1 Lean Meat, 3 Fat ❧ **Carbohydrate Choices:** 3

Fast Veggie Sides

Serving plain cooked frozen or fresh vegetables is always an option, but in a few extra minutes, you can "doctor" veggies to make some really decent sides!

1 **Green Beans with Shaved Asiago:** Drizzle hot cooked green beans with extra-virgin olive oil, then, holding your vegetable peeler over the beans, shave slices of Asiago or Parmesan cheese on top.

2 **Asparagus with Toasted Nuts and Citrus Zest:** Top hot cooked asparagus spears with slivered almonds or pine nuts that have been toasted in melted butter on top of the stove. Sprinkle with grated lemon or orange peel.

3 **Broccoli with Garlic-and-Herb Cream Sauce:** Heat garlic-and-herb spreadable cheese in a small saucepan over low heat, stirring frequently, until smooth and creamy, adding milk or cream if needed. Spoon over hot cooked broccoli.

4 Grape Tomato Sauté: Sauté whole grape tomatoes, jarred chopped garlic and Italian seasoning in extra-virgin olive oil just until tomatoes are hot. Season with salt and pepper to taste.

5 Maple-Glazed Carrots: Mix together equal amounts of maple syrup and melted butter; toss with hot cooked, well-drained baby carrots.

6 Cheesy Corn: Mix together hot cooked corn and any flavor of process cheese sauce or salsa con queso dip; heat until hot.

7 Ranch Veggies: Drizzle hot cooked veggies with ranch dressing.

8 Broccoli Italiano: Toss hot cooked broccoli florets with warmed zesty Italian dressing; sprinkle with grated Parmesan cheese or shredded Cheddar cheese.

9 Cheesy Taco Broccoli: Toss hot cooked broccoli florets with shredded taco-flavored cheese; sprinkle with crushed nacho-flavored tortilla chips.

10 Sugar Snap Peas with Honey Butter: Mix together equal amounts of honey and melted butter; toss with hot cooked, well-drained sugar snap peas. Sprinkle with honey-roasted peanuts.

This icon means: 🕐 20 minutes or less

Prep Time **20 Minutes**
Start to Finish **20 Minutes**

Taco Chicken with Corn Salsa

1 package (1.25 oz) taco seasoning mix

4 boneless skinless chicken breasts
(about 1 1/4 lb)

2 tablespoons vegetable oil

1 can (11 oz) whole kernel corn
with red and green peppers,
drained

1 medium avocado, pitted, peeled and
chopped

2 tablespoons finely chopped red onion

2 tablespoons chopped fresh cilantro

1 tablespoon lime juice

1 teaspoon honey

1   In medium bowl, reserve 2 teaspoons of the taco seasoning mix. Coat chicken with remaining taco seasoning mix.

2   In 12-inch skillet, heat oil over medium heat. Cook chicken in oil 3 to 5 minutes, turning once, until brown. Reduce heat to medium-low. Cook about 8 minutes, turning once, until juice of chicken is clear when center of thickest part is cut (170°F).

3   Meanwhile, add remaining ingredients to reserved taco seasoning mix; toss gently. Serve salsa with chicken.

4 servings

Instant **Success!**

This lively little salsa can be made ahead of time, but be sure to add the avocado just before serving to preserve its color and texture.

1 Serving: Calories 410 (Calories from Fat 170); Total Fat 18g (Saturated Fat 3.5g; Trans Fat 0g); Cholesterol 85mg; Sodium 690mg; Total Carbohydrate 26g (Dietary Fiber 5g; Sugars 10g); Protein 35g ✌ **% Daily Value:** Vitamin A 15%; Vitamin C 10%; Calcium 4%; Iron 10% ✌ **Exchanges:** 1 Starch, 1/2 Other Carbohydrate, 4 1/2 Very Lean Meat, 3 Fat ✌ **Carbohydrate Choices:** 2

Betty Crocker quick & easy cookbook

Tuscan Rosemary Chicken and White Beans

Prep Time **30 Minutes**
Start to Finish **30 Minutes**

1/3 cup Italian dressing

4 boneless skinless chicken breasts
(about 1 1/4 lb)

1/4 cup water

2 medium carrots, sliced (1 cup)

2 medium stalks celery, sliced (1 cup)

1/4 cup coarsely chopped drained
sun-dried tomatoes in oil

1 teaspoon dried rosemary leaves,
crushed

1 can (19 oz) cannellini beans, drained,
rinsed

1 In 12-inch skillet, heat dressing over medium-high heat. Cook chicken in dressing 2 to 3 minutes on each side or until lightly browned.

2 Reduce heat to medium-low. Add water, carrots, celery, tomatoes and rosemary to skillet. Cover; simmer about 10 minutes or until carrots are crisp-tender and juice of chicken is clear when center of thickest part is cut (170°F).

3 Stir in beans. Cover; cook 5 to 6 minutes or until beans are thoroughly heated.

4 servings

Easy Add-On

The flavorful pan juices are just begging to be soaked up with a hunk of crusty bread!

1 Serving: Calories 440 (Calories from Fat 130); Total Fat 14g (Saturated Fat 2g; Trans Fat 0g); Cholesterol 90mg; Sodium 320mg; Total Carbohydrate 34g (Dietary Fiber 9g; Sugars 5g); Protein 43g ❧ **% Daily Value:** Vitamin A 80%; Vitamin C 8%; Calcium 15%; Iron 30% ❧ **Exchanges:** 2 Starch, 1 Vegetable, 5 Very Lean Meat, 2 Fat ❧ **Carbohydrate Choices:** 2

Southwestern Chicken Scaloppine

4 boneless skinless chicken breast halves (about 1 1/4 lb)

1/4 cup all-purpose flour

1 teaspoon ground cumin

1/2 teaspoon salt

2 tablespoons vegetable oil

1/2 cup chicken broth

1/4 teaspoon red pepper sauce, if desired

2 tablespoons lime juice

2 tablespoons chopped fresh cilantro

1 Between pieces of plastic wrap or waxed paper, place chicken breast half with smooth side down; gently pound with flat side of meat mallet or rolling pin until about 1/4 inch thick. Repeat with remaining chicken. Cut chicken into smaller pieces if desired.

2 In shallow dish, mix flour, cumin and salt. Coat chicken with flour mixture. Reserve 1 teaspoon flour mixture.

3 In 12-inch nonstick skillet, heat oil over medium heat. Add chicken; cook 3 to 5 minutes on each side or until golden brown and no longer pink in center. Remove chicken from skillet; cover to keep warm.

4 In small bowl, stir reserved 1 teaspoon flour mixture into broth. Gradually stir broth mixture and red pepper sauce into skillet. Heat to boiling; stir in lime juice and cilantro. Serve sauce over chicken.

4 servings

Make it a Meal

Cobble together some cornbread or corn muffins, steamed broccoli and fresh fruit for a scrumptious dinner.

1 Serving: Calories 260 (Calories from Fat 110); Total Fat 12g (Saturated Fat 2.5g; Trans Fat 0g); Cholesterol 85mg; Sodium 500mg; Total Carbohydrate 7g (Dietary Fiber 0g; Sugars 0g); Protein 33g ✒ **% Daily Value:** Vitamin A 0%; Vitamin C 0%; Calcium 2%; Iron 10% ✒ **Exchanges:** 1/2 Other Carbohydrate, 4 1/2 Very Lean Meat, 2 Fat ✒ **Carbohydrate Choices:** 1/2

Two-Pepper Chicken with Honey Butter

4 boneless skinless chicken breasts
   (about 1 1/4 lb)

1 tablespoon black peppercorns, crushed

1 tablespoon white peppercorns, crushed

1 tablespoon vegetable oil

1/4 cup butter or margarine, softened

2 tablespoons honey

1 Coat both sides of chicken with peppercorns. In 10-inch skillet, heat oil over medium-high heat. Cook chicken in oil 15 to 20 minutes, turning once, until juice of chicken is clear when center of thickest part is cut (170°F).

2 In small bowl, mix butter and honey. Top chicken with honey butter.

4 servings

Instant
Success!

How do you crush peppercorns? If you don't have a pepper mill, it's easy using a mortar and pestle, mini-food processor, or spice or coffee grinder. The low-tech method is to place them in a resealable plastic bag and pound with a meat mallet or rolling pin.

1 Serving: Calories 340 (Calories from Fat 180); Total Fat 20g (Saturated Fat 9g; Trans Fat 1g); Cholesterol 115mg; Sodium 160mg; Total Carbohydrate 10g (Dietary Fiber 0g; Sugars 9g); Protein 31g ❧ **% Daily Value:** Vitamin A 8%; Vitamin C 0%; Calcium 2%; Iron 8% ❧ **Exchanges:** 1/2 Other Carbohydrate, 4 1/2 Very Lean Meat, 3 1/2 Fat ❧ Carbohydrate Choices: 1/2

Betty Crocker quick & easy cookbook

Moroccan Spiced Chicken

1 tablespoon paprika

1/2 teaspoon salt

1/2 teaspoon ground cumin

1/4 teaspoon ground allspice

1/4 teaspoon ground cinnamon

4 boneless skinless chicken breasts
(about 1 1/4 lb)

1 tablespoon vegetable oil

2 cups water

1 teaspoon vegetable oil

1 1/2 cups uncooked couscous

1/4 cup raisins, if desired

1 small papaya, peeled, seeded and sliced

1 In small bowl, mix paprika, salt, cumin, allspice and cinnamon. Coat both sides of chicken with spice mixture.

2 In 10-inch skillet, heat 1 tablespoon oil over medium heat. Cook chicken in oil 15 to 20 minutes, turning once, until juice of chicken is clear when center of thickest part is cut (170°F).

3 Meanwhile, in 2-quart saucepan, heat water and 1 teaspoon oil just to boiling. Stir in couscous; remove from heat. Cover; let stand 5 minutes. Fluff couscous before serving; stir in raisins. Serve chicken with couscous and papaya.

4 servings

Make it a Meal

Looking for something quick but fancy to serve guests? Dress up this dish with warmed pita folds drizzled with olive oil or melted butter or with Middle Eastern flatbread.

1 Serving: Calories 470 (Calories from Fat 90); Total Fat 10g (Saturated Fat 2g; Trans Fat 0g); Cholesterol 85mg; Sodium 380mg; Total Carbohydrate 55g (Dietary Fiber 5g; Sugars 4g); Protein 40g ✧ **% Daily Value:** Vitamin A 25%; Vitamin C 20%; Calcium 4%; Iron 15% ✧ **Exchanges:** 3 1/2 Starch, 4 1/2 Very Lean Meat, 1 Fat ✧ **Carbohydrate Choices:** 3 1/2

Chicken in Fresh Herbs

4 boneless skinless chicken breasts (about 1 1/4 lb)

1 medium shallot, chopped

1/4 cup chopped fresh chervil leaves

1/4 cup chopped fresh tarragon leaves

1/2 cup dry white wine or chicken broth

1 tablespoon lemon juice

1/2 teaspoon salt

Cracked pepper, if desired

1 Heat 10-inch skillet over medium-high heat until hot.

2 Cook all ingredients except pepper in skillet 15 to 20 minutes, turning chicken once, until juice of chicken is clear when center of thickest part is cut (170°F). Sprinkle with pepper.

4 servings

Instant **Success!**

This farmers' market–fresh dish uses chervil, an herb with a sweet flavor reminiscent of onion and parsley. It looks very similar to Italian flat-leaf parsley, which can be used as a substitute. The tarragon has a delicate licorice flavor.

1 Serving: Calories 170 (Calories from Fat 40); Total Fat 4.5g (Saturated Fat 1.5g; Trans Fat 0g); Cholesterol 85mg; Sodium 380mg; Total Carbohydrate 0g (Dietary Fiber 0g; Sugars 0g); Protein 31g ☙ **% Daily Value:** Vitamin A 10%; Vitamin C 6%; Calcium 2%; Iron 8% ☙ **Exchanges:** 4 1/2 Very Lean Meat, 1/2 Fat ☙ **Carbohydrate Choices:** 0

Feta-Topped Chicken

4 boneless skinless chicken breasts (about 1 1/4 lb)

2 tablespoons balsamic vinaigrette dressing

1 teaspoon Italian seasoning

1/4 teaspoon seasoned pepper

1 large plum (Roma) tomato, cut into 8 slices

1/4 cup crumbled feta cheese (1 oz)

1 Set oven control to broil. Brush both sides of chicken breasts with dressing. Sprinkle both sides with Italian seasoning and seasoned pepper. Place on rack in broiler pan.

2 Broil with tops 4 inches from heat about 10 minutes, turning once, until juice of chicken is clear when center of thickest part is cut (170°F). Top with tomato and cheese. Broil 2 to 3 minutes longer or until cheese is lightly browned.

4 servings

Make it a Meal

Boil up some orzo pasta while the chicken is cooking. Toss the hot pasta with a little of the dressing, or drizzle with olive oil and sprinkle with garlic salt before tossing.

1 Serving: Calories 230 (Calories from Fat 80); Total Fat 9g (Saturated Fat 2.5g; Trans Fat 0g); Cholesterol 95mg; Sodium 230mg; Total Carbohydrate 3g (Dietary Fiber 0g; Sugars 2g); Protein 33g ✄ **% Daily Value:** Vitamin A 10%; Vitamin C 4%; Calcium 6%; Iron 8% ✄ **Exchanges:** 4 1/2 Very Lean Meat, 1 1/2 Fat ✄ **Carbohydrate Choices:** 0

Barbecue Chicken and Vegetable Supper

1 tablespoon vegetable oil

4 boneless skinless chicken breasts
(about 1 1/4 lb)

1/2 teaspoon salt

2 cups frozen whole green beans
(from 14-oz bag)

2 cups refrigerated red potato wedges
(from 20-oz bag)

1 jar (12 oz) chicken gravy

1/3 cup barbecue sauce

1 In 12-inch nonstick skillet, heat oil over medium-high heat. Add chicken; sprinkle with salt. Cook 4 minutes, turning once, until browned.

2 Add beans, potatoes, gravy and barbecue sauce; stir to coat and mix. Cover; cook 5 to 8 minutes, stirring occasionally, until beans and potatoes are tender and juice of chicken is clear when center of thickest part is cut (170°F).

4 servings

Instant
Success!

Gravy lovers, this saucy skillet supper is your meal ticket! Try substituting frozen potato wedges or steak fries (no need to thaw first!) if you can't find the refrigerated potato wedges.

1 Serving: Calories 400 (Calories from Fat 120); Total Fat 13g (Saturated Fat 3g; Trans Fat 0g); Cholesterol 85mg; Sodium 1220mg; Total Carbohydrate 33g (Dietary Fiber 6g; Sugars 11g); Protein 37g ❧ **% Daily Value:** Vitamin A 8%; Vitamin C 6%; Calcium 6%; Iron 15% ❧ **Exchanges:** 1 Starch, 1 Other Carbohydrate, 1 Vegetable, 4 1/2 Very Lean Meat, 2 Fat ❧ **Carbohydrate Choices:** 2

Chicken with Mushrooms and Carrots

4 slices bacon, chopped

4 boneless skinless chicken breasts
(about 1 1/4 lb)

1/4 teaspoon pepper

2 cups ready-to-eat baby-cut carrots

1 cup chicken broth

1/4 cup dry white wine or chicken broth

1 tablespoon cornstarch

1/2 teaspoon dried thyme leaves

1/4 teaspoon salt

4 oz small fresh mushrooms, cut in half
(about 1 1/3 cups)

1 In 12-inch nonstick skillet, cook bacon over medium heat 6 to 8 minutes, stirring occasionally, until crisp. Remove bacon to paper towel to drain.

2 Add chicken to bacon drippings in skillet; sprinkle with pepper. Cook over medium heat 4 to 5 minutes, turning once, until well browned. Add carrots and 1/4 cup of the broth. Cover; cook 7 to 9 minutes or until carrots are crisp-tender and juice of chicken is clear when center of thickest part is cut (170°F).

3 Meanwhile, to remaining chicken broth, add wine, cornstarch, thyme and salt; mix well. Add broth mixture and mushrooms to skillet. Cook 3 to 5 minutes, stirring once or twice, until bubbly. Cover; cook about 3 minutes longer or until mushrooms are tender. Sprinkle with bacon.

4 servings

Speed it Up

To make this luscious chicken recipe even faster, buy presliced mushrooms and toss them straight into the skillet.

1 Serving: Calories 260 (Calories from Fat 80); Total Fat 8g (Saturated Fat 2.5g; Trans Fat 0g); Cholesterol 95mg; Sodium 710mg; Total Carbohydrate 9g (Dietary Fiber 2g; Sugars 3g); Protein 37g ✽ **% Daily Value:** Vitamin A 150%; Vitamin C 4%; Calcium 4%; Iron 10% ✽ **Exchanges:** 1/2 Other Carbohydrate, 1 Vegetable, 5 Very Lean Meat, 1 Fat ✽ **Carbohydrate Choices:** 1/2

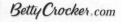

Chicken Alfredo over Biscuits

1 tablespoon vegetable oil

1/2 teaspoon dried thyme leaves

1/4 teaspoon salt

1/4 teaspoon pepper

1 lb boneless skinless chicken breasts, cut into 1-inch pieces

1 bag (1 lb) frozen mixed vegetables

1 container (10 oz) refrigerated Alfredo pasta sauce

1/2 teaspoon Dijon mustard

8 baking powder biscuits

1 In 10-inch nonstick skillet, heat oil, thyme, salt and pepper over medium-high heat. Cook chicken in oil mixture, stirring occasionally, until no longer pink in center.

2 Stir in remaining ingredients except biscuits; reduce heat to medium. Cover; cook 5 to 6 minutes, stirring occasionally, until hot.

3 Split open biscuits. Serve chicken mixture over biscuits.

4 servings

Make it a Meal

Ah, comfort food—with a quick twist! If you do have a few extra minutes, add a cup of sliced celery in step 1 for crunch. A side dish is as simple as sliced apples and pears sprinkled with nuts and a dash of cinnamon.

1 **Serving:** Calories 720 (Calories from Fat 340); Total Fat 38g (Saturated Fat 18g; Trans Fat 2.5g); Cholesterol 140mg; Sodium 1340mg; Total Carbohydrate 55g (Dietary Fiber 6g; Sugars 10g); Protein 38g ✌ **% Daily Value:** Vitamin A 110%; Vitamin C 4%; Calcium 35%; Iron 20% ✌ **Exchanges:** 2 Starch, 1 1/2 Other Carbohydrate, 4 1/2 Very Lean Meat, 7 Fat ✌ **Carbohydrate Choices:** 3 1/2

Extra-Easy Pad Thai–Style Chicken

Prep Time **20 Minutes**
Start to Finish **20 Minutes**

1 tablespoon vegetable oil

1 lb uncooked chicken breast tenders
    (not breaded), cut in half crosswise

2 eggs, beaten

2 cups water

2 packages (3 oz each) chili-flavor
    ramen noodles

1/4 cup lime juice

4 medium green onions, sliced
    (1/4 cup)

1/2 cup chopped salted peanuts

4 teaspoons chopped fresh cilantro

1 In 12-inch nonstick skillet, heat oil over medium-high heat. Cook chicken in oil 4 to 5 minutes, stirring frequently, until browned. Stir in eggs. Cook 2 to 3 minutes, stirring occasionally, until eggs are firm.

2 Stir in water, noodles with contents of seasoning packets and lime juice. Cover; cook 5 minutes, stirring once or twice to separate noodles.

3 Stir to mix all ingredients; spoon onto serving plates. Sprinkle with onions, peanuts and cilantro.

4 servings

Instant Success!

If you can't find the chili-flavor ramen noodles in your neck of the woods, try chicken-, shrimp- or vegetable-flavor. Fish sauce is often used in traditional pad thai; if you'd like to try it, replace 2 tablespoons of the water with fish sauce.

1 Serving: Calories 490 (Calories from Fat 220); Total Fat 25g (Saturated Fat 5g; Trans Fat 2.5g); Cholesterol 155mg; Sodium 930mg; Total Carbohydrate 30g (Dietary Fiber 4g; Sugars 2g); Protein 37g ✦ **% Daily Value:** Vitamin A 10%; Vitamin C 6%; Calcium 4%; Iron 10% ✦ **Exchanges:** 2 Starch, 4 1/2 Lean Meat, 2 Fat ✦ **Carbohydrate Choices:** 2

Prep Time **30 Minutes**

Start to Finish **30 Minutes**

Grilled Chicken Breasts with Tomato-Basil Butter

6 boneless skinless chicken breasts (about 1 3/4 lb)

2 teaspoons garlic-pepper blend

1/2 cup butter or margarine, softened

1 tablespoon chopped fresh or 1 teaspoon dried basil leaves

3 tablespoons tomato paste

1 Brush grill rack with vegetable oil. Heat gas or charcoal grill. Sprinkle chicken with garlic-pepper blend.

2 Place chicken on grill. Cover grill; cook over medium heat 15 to 20 minutes, turning once, until juice of chicken is clear when center of thickest part is cut (170°F).

3 In small bowl, mix remaining ingredients. Serve chicken topped with butter mixture.

6 servings

Instant Success!

Don't want to waste tomato paste when a recipe calls for a small amount? Use the squeeze tube version that can be refrigerated after being opened. Or spoon extra canned tomato paste in 1-tablespoon-size dollops on a foil-lined cookie sheet and freeze until solid, then store in a resealable plastic bag in the freezer.

1 Serving: Calories 300 (Calories from Fat 180); Total Fat 20g (Saturated Fat 11g; Trans Fat 1g); Cholesterol 120mg; Sodium 250mg; Total Carbohydrate 2g (Dietary Fiber 0g; Sugars 1g); Protein 30g ✧ **% Daily Value:** Vitamin A 15%; Vitamin C 0%; Calcium 2%; Iron 8% ✧ **Exchanges:** 4 Very Lean Meat, 3 1/2 Fat ✧ **Carbohydrate Choices:** 0

Betty Crocker quick & easy cookbook

Grilled Sesame-Ginger Chicken

Prep Time **25 Minutes**
Start to Finish **25 Minutes**

2 tablespoons teriyaki sauce

1 tablespoon sesame seed, toasted

1 teaspoon ground ginger

4 boneless skinless chicken breasts (about 1 1/4 lb)

1 Brush grill rack with vegetable oil. Heat gas or charcoal grill. In small bowl, mix teriyaki sauce, sesame seed and ginger.

2 Place chicken on grill. Cover grill; cook over medium heat 15 to 20 minutes, brushing frequently with sauce mixture and turning after 10 minutes, until juice of chicken is clear when center of thickest part is cut (170°F). Discard any remaining sauce mixture.

4 servings

Instant
Success!

To toast sesame seed, cook in an ungreased heavy skillet over medium-low heat 5 to 7 minutes, stirring frequently until browning begins, then stirring constantly until golden brown.

1 Serving: Calories 190 (Calories from Fat 50); Total Fat 6g (Saturated Fat 1.5g; Trans Fat 0g); Cholesterol 85mg; Sodium 420mg; Total Carbohydrate 2g (Dietary Fiber 0g; Sugars 1g); Protein 32g ✒ **% Daily Value:** Vitamin A 0%; Vitamin C 0%; Calcium 2%; Iron 8% ✒ **Exchanges:** 4 1/2 Very Lean Meat, 1 Fat ✒ **Carbohydrate Choices:** 0

Grilled Raspberry-Glazed Chicken

1/2 cup raspberry jam

1 tablespoon Dijon mustard

6 boneless skinless chicken breasts
(about 1 3/4 lb)

1 1/2 cups fresh or frozen (thawed and drained) raspberries

1 Brush grill rack with vegetable oil. Heat gas or charcoal grill. In small bowl, mix jam and mustard.

2 Place chicken on grill. Cover grill; cook over medium heat 15 to 20 minutes, brushing occasionally with jam mixture and turning once, until juice of chicken is clear when center of thickest part is cut (170°F). Discard any remaining jam mixture.

3 Serve chicken topped with raspberries.

6 servings

Make it a Meal

It's patio perfect! This fruity grilled chicken goes nicely with coleslaw and garlic bread. Watermelon wedges and frozen pops cool things off for dessert.

1 Serving: Calories 250 (Calories from Fat 40); Total Fat 4.5g (Saturated Fat 1g; Trans Fat 0g); Cholesterol 80mg; Sodium 140mg; Total Carbohydrate 22g (Dietary Fiber 2g; Sugars 14g); Protein 30g ✦ **% Daily Value:** Vitamin A 0%; Vitamin C 8%; Calcium 2%; Iron 8% ✦ **Exchanges:** 1/2 Fruit, 1 Other Carbohydrate, 4 Very Lean Meat, 1/2 Fat ✦ **Carbohydrate Choices:** 1 1/2

Betty Crocker quick & easy cookbook

Grilled Cheddar-Stuffed Chicken Breasts

4 boneless skinless chicken breasts
(about 1 1/4 lb)

1/4 teaspoon salt

1/4 teaspoon pepper

1 piece (3 oz) Cheddar cheese

1 tablespoon butter or margarine, melted

1/4 cup chunky-style salsa

1 Heat gas or charcoal grill. Between pieces of plastic wrap or waxed paper, place each chicken breast smooth side down; gently pound with flat side of meat mallet or rolling pin until about 1/4 inch thick. Sprinkle with salt and pepper.

2 Cut cheese into 4 slices, about 3 × 1 × 1/4 inch. Place 1 slice cheese on center of each chicken piece. Roll chicken around cheese, folding in sides. Secure with toothpicks. Brush rolls with butter.

3 Place chicken rolls, seam sides down, on grill. Cover grill; cook over medium heat about 15 minutes, turning after 10 minutes, until chicken is no longer pink in center. Remove toothpicks before serving. Serve with salsa.

4 servings

Make it a Meal

Enjoy these chicken rolls with deli coleslaw and hot cooked instant rice tossed with black beans. The rice can cook at the same time as the chicken!

1 Serving: Calories 280 (Calories from Fat 130); Total Fat 15g (Saturated Fat 8g; Trans Fat 0g); Cholesterol 115mg; Sodium 450mg; Total Carbohydrate 1g (Dietary Fiber 0g; Sugars 0g); Protein 37g ❧ **% Daily Value:** Vitamin A 8%; Vitamin C 0%; Calcium 15%; Iron 8% ❧ **Exchanges:** 5 Very Lean Meat, 2 1/2 Fat ❧ **Carbohydrate Choices:** 0

Betty Crocker quick & easy cookbook

Grilled Maple- and Cranberry-Glazed Chicken

Prep Time **25 Minutes**
Start to Finish **25 Minutes**

1 can (16 oz) whole berry cranberry sauce

1/2 cup maple-flavored syrup

1/2 teaspoon salt

6 boneless skinless chicken breasts (about 1 3/4 lb)

1 Brush grill rack with vegetable oil. Heat gas or charcoal grill. In small bowl, mix half of the cranberry sauce and the syrup; reserve remaining sauce. Sprinkle salt over chicken.

2 Place chicken on grill. Cover grill; cook over medium heat 10 minutes; turn chicken. Cover grill; cook 5 to 10 minutes longer, brushing occasionally with cranberry-syrup mixture, until juice of chicken is clear when center of thickest part is cut (170°F). Serve with remaining cranberry sauce.

6 servings

Make it a Meal

Team this sweetly glazed chicken with your favorite stuffing mix and a convenient form of mashed potatoes like the refrigerated version or one of the flavored instant varieties.

1 Serving: Calories 360 (Calories from Fat 40); Total Fat 4.5g (Saturated Fat 1g; Trans Fat 0g); Cholesterol 80mg; Sodium 320mg; Total Carbohydrate 50g (Dietary Fiber 0g; Sugars 37g); Protein 29g ❧ **% Daily Value:** Vitamin A 0%; Vitamin C 0%; Calcium 0%; Iron 6% ❧ **Exchanges:** 3 1/2 Other Carbohydrate, 4 Very Lean Meat, 1/2 Fat ❧ Carbohydrate Choices: 3

Italian Chopped Salad

6 cups chopped romaine lettuce

1 cup fresh basil leaves

1 cup cut-up rotisserie or other cooked
chicken

2 large tomatoes, chopped (2 cups)

2 medium cucumbers, chopped
(1 1/2 cups)

3 oz Italian salami, chopped

1 can (15 oz) cannellini beans, drained,
rinsed

2/3 cup red wine vinaigrette or Italian
dressing

1 In large bowl, place all ingredients except dressing.

2 Pour dressing over salad; toss until coated.

4 servings

Instant
Success!

*Make this at home? You bet you
can! Many restaurant favorites
are easy to duplicate, such as
this hip version of a chopped
salad. Sprinkle the salad with
shredded or shaved Asiago,
Parmesan or Romano cheese.*

1 Serving: Calories 500 (Calories from Fat 240); Total Fat 27g (Saturated Fat 4.5g; Trans Fat 0g); Cholesterol 55mg;
Sodium 940mg; Total Carbohydrate 36g (Dietary Fiber 10g; Sugars 9g); Protein 27g ✎ **% Daily Value:** Vitamin A
130%; Vitamin C 60%; Calcium 20%; Iron 30% ✎ **Exchanges:** 1 1/2 Starch, 1/2 Other Carbohydrate, 1 Vegetable,
3 Very Lean Meat, 5 Fat ✎ **Carbohydrate Choices:** 2 1/2

Betty Crocker quick & easy cookbook

Grilled Chicken Citrus Salad

2/3 cup citrus vinaigrette dressing

4 boneless skinless chicken breasts
(about 1 1/4 lb)

1 bag (10 oz) ready-to-eat romaine lettuce

2 unpeeled apples, cubed (about 2 cups)

1/2 cup coarsely chopped dried apricots

2 medium green onions, sliced
(2 tablespoons)

1/2 cup chopped honey-roasted
peanuts

1 Heat gas or charcoal grill. Place 2 tablespoons of the dressing in small bowl. Brush all sides of chicken with the 2 tablespoons dressing.

2 In large bowl, toss lettuce, apples, apricots and onions; set aside.

3 Place chicken on grill. Cover grill; cook over medium heat 8 to 10 minutes, turning once, until juice of chicken is clear when center of thickest part is cut (170°F).

4 Add remaining dressing to lettuce mixture; toss. On 4 plates, divide lettuce mixture. Cut chicken crosswise to slices; place on lettuce. Sprinkle with peanuts.

4 servings

Instant
Success!

With so many wonderful prewashed salad greens available, feel free to use your favorite for this recipe.

1 Serving: Calories 550 (Calories from Fat 280); Total Fat 31g (Saturated Fat 4g; Trans Fat 0g); Cholesterol 90mg; Sodium 510mg; Total Carbohydrate 30g (Dietary Fiber 6g; Sugars 23g); Protein 39g ✖ **% Daily Value:** Vitamin A 100%; Vitamin C 35%; Calcium 10%; Iron 15% ✖ **Exchanges:** 1 Fruit, 1/2 Other Carbohydrate, 1 Vegetable, 5 1/2 Very Lean Meat, 5 1/2 Fat ✖ **Carbohydrate Choices:** 2

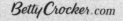

BettyCrocker.com

Sausalito Chicken and Seafood Salad

Prep Time **20 Minutes**
Start to Finish **20 Minutes**

6 cups bite-size pieces assorted salad greens

1 cup diced rotisserie or other cooked chicken

1 large avocado, pitted, peeled and sliced

1 package (8 oz) refrigerated imitation crabmeat chunks

1 can (4 oz) whole green chiles, drained, sliced lengthwise

3/4 cup frozen (thawed) guacamole (from 12-oz container)

1/2 cup sour cream

1 large tomato, chopped (1 cup)

Lime or lemon wedges

1 Among 4 plates, divide salad greens. Top with chicken, avocado, crabmeat and chiles.

2 In small bowl, mix guacamole and sour cream; spoon over salad. Top with tomato. Garnish with lime wedges.

4 servings

Make it a Meal

Sausalito is a quaint town across the bay from San Francisco that's known for its outdoor cafes and wonderful seafood. This refreshing (and refreshingly simple) salad will transport you there!

1 Serving: Calories 360 (Calories from Fat 190); Total Fat 21g (Saturated Fat 6g; Trans Fat 0g); Cholesterol 65mg; Sodium 1400mg; Total Carbohydrate 20g (Dietary Fiber 9g; Sugars 6g); Protein 23g ✂ **% Daily Value:** Vitamin A 110%; Vitamin C 80%; Calcium 10%; Iron 15% ✂ **Exchanges:** 1 Other Carbohydrate, 1 Vegetable, 3 Lean Meat, 2 1/2 Fat ✂ **Carbohydrate Choices:** 1

3 beef & pork

Speedy Potato, Pasta & Rice Sides

Instant potatoes and packaged rice and noodle mixes are wonderful to keep on hand, but if you want a little bit more adventure, try one of these fast and easy ideas.

1 **Chipotle-Cheddar Mashed Potatoes:** Stir chopped canned chipotle chiles in adobo sauce and shredded Cheddar cheese into your mashed potatoes.

2 **Rich and Creamy Roasted Garlic Mashed Potatoes:** Make a package of mashed potatoes seasoned with roasted garlic as directed on the package, except substitute whipping cream or half-and-half for the milk.

3 **Barbecued Steak Fries:** Heat oven as directed on package of frozen steak fries. On foil-lined cookie sheet, arrange fries; spray lightly with cooking spray and sprinkle with barbecue seasoning. Turn fries over and repeat with other side if desired. Bake as directed on package.

4 **Easy Bacon-Cheese Fries:** Heat your favorite type of frozen French fries as directed on the package. Place in shallow serving platter; spoon any flavor warm process cheese sauce or salsa con queso dip over potatoes. Sprinkle with purchased precooked bacon bits and sliced green onion.

5 **Cheesy Pasta:** Toss hot cooked pasta with extra-virgin olive oil and shredded or grated Asiago, Parmesan or Romano cheese. Heat gently if necessary. Sprinkle with dried basil leaves or parsley flakes.

6 **Artichoke Pasta Toss:** Toss hot cooked pasta with a jar (or as many jars as needed) of undrained marinated artichokes (cut into quarters if needed). Heat gently if necessary.

7 **Basil Pasta Toss:** Toss hot cooked pasta with basil pesto; sprinkle with shredded or grated Parmesan cheese. Heat gently if necessary.

8 **Dill and Lemon-Pepper Pasta:** Toss hot cooked pasta with purchased dill dip and a bit of lemon-pepper seasoning. Heat gently if necessary.

9 **Salsa Rice:** Stir salsa and sliced ripe olives into hot cooked rice. Heat gently if necessary; sprinkle with shredded taco-flavored cheese or Cheddar cheese.

10 **Rice Alfredo with Bacon:** Stir purchased Alfredo sauce into hot cooked rice. Heat gently if necessary; sprinkle with precooked bacon bits.

This icon means: 20 minutes or less

Prep Time **10 Minutes**
Start to Finish **20 Minutes**

Strip Steaks with Mango-Peach Salsa

1/4 cup finely chopped red bell pepper

2 teaspoons finely chopped seeded jalapeño chiles

1 teaspoon finely chopped or grated gingerroot or 1/4 teaspoon ground ginger

1/4 cup peach preserves

1 tablespoon lime juice

1 small mango, cut lengthwise in half, pitted and chopped (1 cup)

4 boneless beef New York strip steaks (about 1 1/2 lb)

1 to 2 teaspoons Caribbean jerk seasoning

1 In medium bowl, mix bell pepper, chiles and gingerroot. Stir in preserves, lime juice and mango.

2 Set oven control to broil. Sprinkle both sides of beef with jerk seasoning. Place on rack in broiler pan. Broil with tops 4 to 6 inches from heat 6 to 10 minutes, turning once, until desired doneness. Serve with salsa.

4 servings

Instant
Success!

Fresh mango will be slightly soft to the touch. Cut lengthwise into two pieces, cutting as close to the seed as possible. Make crisscross cuts 1/2 inch apart into mango flesh. Turn each mango half inside out and scrape off the pieces. Canned or jarred mangoes also can be used for this recipe; be sure to drain well before using.

1 Serving: Calories 360 (Calories from Fat 110); Total Fat 12g (Saturated Fat 4.5g; Trans Fat 0.5g); Cholesterol 75mg; Sodium 130mg; Total Carbohydrate 24g (Dietary Fiber 1g; Sugars 17g); Protein 40g ☞ **% Daily Value:** Vitamin A 15%; Vitamin C 60%; Calcium 0%; Iron 20% ☞ **Exchanges:** 1 1/2 Other Carbohydrate, 5 1/2 Very Lean Meat, 2 Fat ☞ **Carbohydrate Choices:** 1 1/2

Grilled Rosemary-Dijon Steaks

Prep Time **20 Minutes**
Start to Finish **20 Minutes**

1/4 cup Dijon mustard

2 teaspoons chopped fresh or
    1/2 teaspoon dried rosemary
    leaves, crushed

1 teaspoon coarsely ground pepper

2 cloves garlic, finely chopped

4 boneless beef top loin steaks, about
    1 inch thick (about 1 1/2 lb)

1   Heat gas or charcoal grill. In small bowl, mix mustard, rosemary, pepper and garlic; spread on both sides of beef.

2   Place beef on grill. Cook uncovered over medium heat 1 minute on each side to seal in juices. Cover grill; cook 8 to 9 minutes longer for medium doneness, turning once.

4 servings

Make it a Meal

Celebrate life's simple pleasures! Serve the steak with grilled corn on the cob and microwaved "baked" potatoes with sour cream and butter.

1 Serving: Calories 190 (Calories from Fat 80); Total Fat 9g (Saturated Fat 3g; Trans Fat 0g); Cholesterol 50mg; Sodium 410mg; Total Carbohydrate 2g (Dietary Fiber 0g; Sugars 0g); Protein 27g ✢ **% Daily Value:** Vitamin A 2%; Vitamin C 0%; Calcium 2%; Iron 15% ✢ **Exchanges:** 4 Lean Meat ✢ **Carbohydrate Choices:** 0

Beef Tenderloin and Mushrooms in Garlic Butter Sauce

6 tablespoons cold butter

4 beef tenderloin steaks, 1 1/2 inches thick (about 1 3/4 lb)

1/2 teaspoon salt

1/4 teaspoon pepper

1 1/2 cups sliced baby portabella mushrooms (about 3.5 oz)

2 cloves garlic, finely chopped

3/4 cup dry white wine or nonalcoholic wine

1 In 10-inch skillet, melt 1 tablespoon of the butter over medium-high heat. Sprinkle beef steaks with salt and pepper. Cook beef in butter 6 to 8 minutes, turning once, until deep brown. Reduce heat to low. Cover; cook 6 to 8 minutes (beef will be almost done and continue to cook while standing). Remove beef to platter; cover to keep warm.

2 Increase heat to medium. Add 1 tablespoon of the remaining butter to skillet. Add mushrooms and garlic. Cook 3 to 4 minutes, stirring once or twice, until tender. Add wine. Cook 4 to 5 minutes, stirring occasionally, until reduced to about one-third and mixture is slightly thick. Remove from heat.

3 Beat remaining butter, 1 tablespoon at a time, into sauce with wire whisk just until melted. Serve mushrooms and sauce over beef.

4 servings

Speed it Up

Love it or hate it, but jarred chopped garlic is a handy-dandy little time-saver! Look for presliced mushrooms for a "chopping-free" meal.

1 Serving: Calories 470 (Calories from Fat 280); Total Fat 31g (Saturated Fat 16g; Trans Fat 1.5g); Cholesterol 130mg; Sodium 480mg; Total Carbohydrate 1g (Dietary Fiber 0g; Sugars 0g); Protein 47g ✎ **% Daily Value:** Vitamin A 10%; Vitamin C 0%; Calcium 2%; Iron 20% ✎ **Exchanges:** 7 Lean Meat, 2 Fat ✎ **Carbohydrate Choices:** 0

Grilled Lemon-Pepper Steaks

4 beef sirloin or rib eye steaks, 1 inch thick (about 2 lb)

1/2 teaspoon garlic salt

1/4 cup butter or margarine, melted

2 tablespoons chopped fresh or 1 tablespoon dried basil leaves

2 teaspoons lemon-pepper seasoning

2 medium bell peppers (any color), cut lengthwise in half, seeded

1 Spray grill rack with cooking spray. Heat gas or charcoal grill.

2 Trim fat on beef steaks to 1/2-inch thickness if necessary. Sprinkle garlic salt over beef. In small bowl, mix butter, basil and lemon-pepper seasoning; brush over beef and bell pepper halves.

3 Place beef and bell peppers on grill. Cover grill; cook over medium heat 10 to 15 minutes for medium beef doneness, turning once. Brush tops of steaks with butter mixture. Cut bell peppers into strips. Serve over beef.

4 servings

Instant **Success!**

Keep your steaks nice and juicy! Make sure the grill is hot before adding the steaks. A hot grill quickly sears the outside of the meat, sealing in the juices.

1 Serving: Calories 360 (Calories from Fat 160); Total Fat 18g (Saturated Fat 9g; Trans Fat 1g); Cholesterol 145mg; Sodium 430mg; Total Carbohydrate 4g (Dietary Fiber 1g; Sugars 2g); Protein 46g ✒ **% Daily Value:** Vitamin A 15%; Vitamin C 40%; Calcium 0%; Iron 25% ✒ **Exchanges:** 1 Vegetable, 6 1/2 Lean Meat ✒ **Carbohydrate Choices:** 0

Grilled Hamburgers with Roasted Sweet Onions

Prep Time **25** Minutes
Start to Finish **25** Minutes

Cooking spray

4 lean ground beef patties (4 to 6 oz each)

2 tablespoons steak sauce

1 package (1 oz) onion soup mix
(from 2-oz box)

2 large Bermuda or other sweet onions,
cut in half, then thinly sliced and
separated (6 cups)

2 tablespoons packed brown sugar

1 tablespoon balsamic vinegar

1 Heat gas or charcoal grill. Cut 2 (12 × 8-inch) sheets of heavy-duty foil;
spray with cooking spray. Brush beef patties with steak sauce; sprinkle with
half of the soup mix (dry).

2 Place half of the onions on center of each foil sheet. Sprinkle with remaining
soup mix, brown sugar and vinegar. Bring up 2 sides of foil so edges meet.
Seal edges, making tight 1/2-inch fold; fold again, allowing space for circulation
and expansion. Fold other sides to seal.

3 Place packets and beef patties on grill. Cover grill; cook over medium heat
10 to 15 minutes, turning patties and rotating packets 1/2 turn once or twice,
until meat thermometer inserted in center of patties reads 160°F. To serve
onions, cut large X across top of each packet; carefully fold back foil to allow
steam to escape. Serve onions with patties.

4 servings

Make it a Meal

*Everything tastes better grilled!
Lightly grill some hamburger
buns for added crunchiness.
Throw some frozen fries in the
oven before starting the recipe.
You'll be chowing down in no time!*

1 Serving: Calories 320 (Calories from Fat 120); Total Fat 13g (Saturated Fat 5g; Trans Fat 1g); Cholesterol 70mg;
Sodium 790mg; Total Carbohydrate 30g (Dietary Fiber 4g; Sugars 17g); Protein 22g ✍ **% Daily Value:** Vitamin A 0%;
Vitamin C 15%; Calcium 8%; Iron 15% ✍ **Exchanges:** 1 1/2 Starch, 1 1/2 Vegetable, 2 Medium-Fat Meat, 1/2 Fat
✍ **Carbohydrate Choices:** 2

Prep Time **20 Minutes**
Start to Finish **20 Minutes**

Monterey Skillet Hamburgers

1 lb lean (at least 80%) ground beef

1 can (4.5 oz) chopped green chiles, drained

2 tablespoons chopped fresh cilantro

1 teaspoon chili powder

1/2 teaspoon salt

1/8 teaspoon ground red pepper (cayenne)

1 medium red onion, thinly sliced

1 medium avocado, pitted, peeled and sliced

4 slices (1 oz each) Monterey Jack cheese

1 In large bowl, mix beef, chiles, cilantro, chili powder, salt and red pepper. Shape mixture into 4 patties, about 1/2 inch thick.

2 Spray 10-inch skillet with cooking spray; heat over medium-high heat. Cook onion in skillet 1 to 2 minutes, stirring occasionally, just until tender. Remove from skillet.

3 Add beef patties to skillet. Cook 10 to 12 minutes, turning once, until meat thermometer inserted in center of patties reads 160°F. Top patties with onion, avocado and cheese. Cover; heat until cheese is melted.

4 servings

Instant Success!

To get to that luscious avocado quickly, first cut it lengthwise in half around the pit. On a solid surface and with your other hand out of the way, hit the pit with the blade of a sharp knife so it sticks, then twist the knife to easily remove the pit from the avocado. Carefully remove the pit from the knife with a paper towel because it's very slippery. Peel off the leathery skin with your fingers.

1 Serving: Calories 400 (Calories from Fat 250); Total Fat 28g (Saturated Fat 11g; Trans Fat 1g); Cholesterol 95mg; Sodium 980mg; Total Carbohydrate 8g (Dietary Fiber 4g; Sugars 3g); Protein 28g ✎ % Daily Value: Vitamin A 20%; Vitamin C 8%; Calcium 25%; Iron 20% ✎ Exchanges: 1/2 Other Carbohydrate, 4 Medium-Fat Meat, 1 1/2 Fat ✎ Carbohydrate Choices: 1/2

Mini Meat Loaves

1/2 cup ketchup

2 tablespoons packed brown sugar

1 lb lean (at least 80%) ground beef

1/2 lb ground pork

1/2 cup Original Bisquick mix

1/4 teaspoon pepper

1 small onion, finely chopped (1/4 cup)

1 egg

1 Heat oven to 450°F. In small bowl, stir ketchup and brown sugar until mixed; reserve 1/4 cup for topping. In large bowl, stir remaining ingredients and remaining ketchup mixture until well mixed.

2 Spray 13 × 9-inch pan with cooking spray. Place meat mixture in pan; pat into 12 × 4-inch rectangle. Cut lengthwise down center and then crosswise into sixths to form 12 loaves. Separate loaves, using spatula, so no edges are touching. Brush loaves with reserved 1/4 cup ketchup mixture.

3 Bake 18 to 20 minutes or until loaves are no longer pink in center and meat thermometer inserted in center of loaves reads 160°F.

6 servings (2 loaves each)

Speed it Up

These cute little loaves bake much faster than a traditional whole loaf, plus you get more of that tangy crust. Stick with the "mini" theme by serving small boiled potatoes and cooked baby-cut carrots (both of which also cook up extra-fast!).

1 Serving: Calories 300 (Calories from Fat 140); Total Fat 16g (Saturated Fat 6g; Trans Fat 1g); Cholesterol 105mg; Sodium 430mg; Total Carbohydrate 16g (Dietary Fiber 0g; Sugars 10g); Protein 22g ✍ **% Daily Value:** Vitamin A 4%; Vitamin C 2%; Calcium 4%; Iron 10% ✍ **Exchanges:** 1/2 Starch, 1/2 Other Carbohydrate, 3 Medium-Fat Meat ✍ **Carbohydrate Choices:** 1

Beef Fajita Bowls

1 cup uncooked regular long-grain
white rice

1 lb boneless beef sirloin steak

2 tablespoons vegetable oil

1 flour tortilla (8 inch), cut into
4 × 1/2-inch strips

1 bag (1 lb) frozen bell pepper and
onion stir-fry

1/2 cup frozen whole kernel corn
(from 1-lb bag)

1 cup chunky-style salsa

2 tablespoons lime juice

2 tablespoons chili sauce

1/2 teaspoon ground cumin

2 tablespoons chopped fresh cilantro

1 Cook rice as directed on package. Meanwhile, cut beef with grain into
2-inch strips; cut strips across grain into 1/8-inch slices. (Beef is easier to cut
if partially frozen, 30 to 60 minutes.)

2 Heat 12-inch nonstick skillet over medium-high heat. Add oil; rotate skillet
to coat bottom. Cook tortilla strips in oil 1 to 2 minutes on each side, adding
additional oil if necessary, until golden brown and crisp. Drain on paper towel.

3 Add beef to skillet; stir-fry over medium-high heat 4 to 5 minutes or until
beef is brown; remove beef from skillet. Add frozen bell pepper mixture and
corn to skillet; stir-fry 1 minute. Cover; cook 2 to 3 minutes, stirring twice, until
crisp-tender. Stir in beef, salsa, lime juice, chili sauce and cumin. Cook 2 to 3
minutes, stirring occasionally, until hot. Stir in cilantro. Among 4 bowls, divide
rice. Top with beef mixture and tortilla strips.

4 servings

Speed it Up

*You'll be "bowl-ed" over by this
super-easy twist on fajitas.
To make this even quicker, top
with packaged tortilla chips
instead. Then reduce the
amount of oil for sautéing
the beef to 1 tablespoon.*

1 Serving: Calories 510 (Calories from Fat 110); Total Fat 12g (Saturated Fat 2.5g; Trans Fat 0g); Cholesterol 65mg;
Sodium 1030mg; Total Carbohydrate 66g (Dietary Fiber 4g; Sugars 8g); Protein 33g ❧ **% Daily Value:** Vitamin A 15%;
Vitamin C 50%; Calcium 8%; Iron 30% ❧ **Exchanges:** 3 1/2 Starch, 1/2 Other Carbohydrate, 1 Vegetable, 3 Lean
Meat ❧ **Carbohydrate Choices:** 4 1/2

Ramen-Beef Stir-Fry

Prep Time **25 Minutes**
Start to Finish **25 Minutes**

1 lb boneless beef sirloin

2 cups water

1 package (3 oz) Oriental-flavor ramen
   noodle soup mix

1 bag (14 to 16 oz) fresh stir-fry
   vegetables

1/4 cup stir-fry sauce

1 Cut beef into thin strips. Spray 12-inch skillet with cooking spray; heat over medium-high heat. Cook beef in skillet 3 to 5 minutes, stirring occasionally, until brown. Remove beef from skillet.

2 In same skillet, heat water to boiling. Break block of noodles from soup mix into water; stir until slightly softened. Stir in vegetables. Heat to boiling. Boil 4 to 5 minutes, stirring occasionally, until vegetables are crisp-tender.

3 Stir in contents of seasoning packet from soup mix, stir-fry sauce and beef. Cook 2 to 3 minutes, stirring frequently, until hot.

4 servings

Instant
Success!

This trick is a keeper! Beef is easier to cut if partially frozen, for 30 to 60 minutes. Quick-cooking ramen noodles, containing the seasoning packet, are perfect for fast dishes because you don't have to add a lot of ingredients for flavor.

1 Serving: Calories 290 (Calories from Fat 70); Total Fat 8g (Saturated Fat 2.5g; Trans Fat 1.5g); Cholesterol 65mg; Sodium 1150mg; Total Carbohydrate 23g (Dietary Fiber 3g; Sugars 5g); Protein 30g ✒ **% Daily Value:** Vitamin A 20%; Vitamin C 30%; Calcium 4%; Iron 20% ✒ **Exchanges:** 1 Starch, 1 Vegetable, 3 1/2 Lean Meat ✒ **Carbohydrate Choices:** 1 1/2

Prep Time **20 Minutes**
Start to Finish **20 Minutes**

Fajita Salad

3/4 lb lean boneless beef sirloin steak

1 tablespoon vegetable oil

2 medium bell peppers, cut into strips

1 small onion, thinly sliced

4 cups bite-size pieces salad greens

1/3 cup Italian dressing

1/4 cup sour cream

1   Cut beef with grain into 2-inch strips; cut strips across grain into 1/8-inch slices. (Beef is easier to cut if partially frozen, 30 to 60 minutes.)

2   In 10-inch nonstick skillet, heat oil over medium-high heat. Cook beef in oil about 3 minutes, stirring occasionally, until brown. Remove beef from skillet.

3   In same skillet, cook bell peppers and onion about 3 minutes, stirring occasionally, until bell peppers are crisp-tender. Stir in beef.

4   On serving platter, place salad greens. Top with beef mixture. In small bowl, mix dressing and sour cream; drizzle over salad.

4 servings

Speed it Up

Check out the meat case for all the precut meats now available. Besides being a time-saver, these meats often come in small, one-time-use portions.

1 Serving: Calories 280 (Calories from Fat 160); Total Fat 17g (Saturated Fat 4g; Trans Fat 0g); Cholesterol 60mg; Sodium 230mg; Total Carbohydrate 9g (Dietary Fiber 2g; Sugars 5g); Protein 22g ✒ **% Daily Value:** Vitamin A 60%; Vitamin C 100%; Calcium 8%; Iron 15% ✒ **Exchanges:** 1 Vegetable, 3 Lean Meat, 2 Fat ✒ **Carbohydrate Choices:** 1/2

Grilled Steak and Potato Salad

Prep Time **30 Minutes**
Start to Finish **30 Minutes**

3/4 lb small red potatoes, cut in half

2/3 cup honey Dijon dressing and marinade

1 boneless beef top sirloin steak, 3/4 inch thick (3/4 lb)

1/4 teaspoon salt

1/4 teaspoon coarsely ground pepper

4 cups bite-size pieces romaine lettuce

2 medium tomatoes, cut into thin wedges

1/2 cup thinly sliced red onion

1 Heat gas or charcoal grill. In 2- or 2 1/2-quart saucepan, place potatoes; add enough water to cover potatoes. Heat to boiling; reduce heat to medium. Cook uncovered 5 to 8 minutes or just until potatoes are tender.

2 Drain potatoes; place in medium bowl. Add 2 tablespoons of the dressing; toss to coat. Place potatoes in grill basket (grill "wok") if desired. Brush beef steak with 1 tablespoon of the dressing; sprinkle with salt and pepper.

3 Place beef and potatoes on grill. Cover grill; cook over medium heat 8 to 15 minutes, turning once, until beef is desired doneness and potatoes are golden brown. Cut beef into thin slices.

4 Among 4 plates, divide lettuce, tomatoes and onion. Top with beef and potatoes; drizzle with remaining dressing. Sprinkle with additional pepper if desired.

4 servings

Easy Add-On

You won't have to twist the arm of blue cheese lovers to agree to a generous sprinkle of crumbled blue or Gorgonzola cheese on top of their salads.

1 Serving: Calories 360 (Calories from Fat 180); Total Fat 20g (Saturated Fat 4g; Trans Fat 0g); Cholesterol 35mg; Sodium 440mg; Total Carbohydrate 25g (Dietary Fiber 4g; Sugars 7g); Protein 22g ✺ **% Daily Value:** Vitamin A 80%; Vitamin C 50%; Calcium 6%; Iron 20% ✺ **Exchanges:** 1/2 Starch, 1 Other Carbohydrate, 1 Vegetable, 2 1/2 Lean Meat, 2 1/2 Fat ✺ **Carbohydrate Choices:** 1 1/2

Taco Supper Skillet

1/2 lb lean (at least 80%) ground beef

1 package (1.25 oz) taco seasoning mix

2 1/4 cups water

1 1/2 cups uncooked wagon wheel pasta
(5 1/2 oz)

1 1/2 cups frozen whole kernel corn
(from 1-lb bag)

1 can (15 oz) pinto or kidney beans,
drained, rinsed

1 medium tomato, chopped (3/4 cup)

1/2 cup sour cream

1 cup shredded Cheddar cheese (4 oz)

1 tablespoon chopped fresh chives,
if desired

1 In 12-inch skillet, cook beef over medium-high heat 5 to 7 minutes, stirring frequently, until brown; drain.

2 Stir seasoning mix, water, uncooked pasta, corn, beans and tomato into beef. Heat to boiling; stir. Reduce heat to medium-low. Cover; cook 10 to 15 minutes, stirring occasionally, until pasta is desired doneness and most of the liquid has been absorbed.

3 Stir in sour cream. Remove from heat. Sprinkle with cheese and chives. Cover; let stand 2 to 3 minutes or until cheese is melted.

4 servings

Make it a Meal

Pair this family-style supper with baked tortilla chips and fresh fruit salad served in lettuce cups. For speed, look for cut-up fresh fruit or jarred fruit in the produce section of the supermarket.

1 Serving: Calories 640 (Calories from Fat 210); Total Fat 23g (Saturated Fat 12g; Trans Fat 1g); Cholesterol 85mg; Sodium 590mg; Total Carbohydrate 73g (Dietary Fiber 12g; Sugars 9g); Protein 34g ✎ **% Daily Value:** Vitamin A 30%; Vitamin C 8%; Calcium 25%; Iron 30% ✎ **Exchanges:** 4 1/2 Starch, 1/2 Other Carbohydrate, 3 Medium-Fat Meat, 1 Fat ✎ **Carbohydrate Choices:** 5

Betty Crocker quick & easy cookbook

Fiesta Taco Salad

1 lb lean (at least 80%) ground beef

1/2 cup taco sauce

6 cups bite-size pieces lettuce

1 medium green bell pepper, cut into strips

2 medium tomatoes, cut into wedges

1/2 cup pitted ripe olives, drained

1 cup corn chips

1 cup shredded Cheddar cheese (4 oz)

1/2 cup Thousand Island dressing

1 In 10-inch skillet, cook beef over medium heat 8 to 10 minutes, stirring occasionally, until brown; drain. Stir in taco sauce. Cook 2 to 3 minutes, stirring occasionally, until heated.

2 In large bowl, toss lettuce, bell pepper, tomatoes, olives and corn chips. Spoon hot beef mixture over lettuce mixture; toss. Sprinkle with cheese. Serve immediately with dressing.

5 servings

Speed it Up

If you thought raw ground beef was a handy freezer item, storing frozen precooked ground beef gets you even closer to a hot dinner anytime. Just brown the beef ahead of time; drain and keep in a covered container in the refrigerator for up to 3 days, or freeze up to 4 months.

1 Serving: Calories 410 (Calories from Fat 270); Total Fat 30g (Saturated Fat 11g; Trans Fat 1g); Cholesterol 85mg; Sodium 710mg; Total Carbohydrate 11g (Dietary Fiber 3g; Sugars 6g); Protein 24g ✧ **% Daily Value:** Vitamin A 25%; Vitamin C 50%; Calcium 20%; Iron 15% ✧ **Exchanges:** 1/2 Other Carbohydrate, 1 Vegetable, 3 Medium-Fat Meat, 3 Fat ✧ **Carbohydrate Choices:** 1

Cheesy Beef Hash

Prep Time **30 Minutes**
Start to Finish **30 Minutes**

1 lb lean (at least 80%) ground beef

1 teaspoon salt

5 cups frozen potatoes O'Brien with onions
    and peppers (from 28-oz bag)

1 medium green bell pepper, chopped
    (1 cup)

1/2 medium red onion, chopped
    (1/2 cup)

1 container (8 oz) Cheddar cold-pack
    cheese food or cheese spread

1 cup shredded Cheddar cheese (4 oz)

1 In 12-inch nonstick skillet, cook beef and salt over medium-high heat 5 to 7 minutes, stirring occasionally, until brown; drain.

2 Stir potatoes into beef; reduce heat to medium-low. Cover; cook about 10 minutes, stirring occasionally, until potatoes are almost tender.

3 Stir in bell pepper and onion. Cover; cook 5 to 10 minutes, stirring occasionally, until tender. Stir in cold-pack cheese food. Cook 1 to 2 minutes, stirring occasionally, until thoroughly heated. Top with shredded cheese.

4 servings (1 1/2 cups each)

Instant
Success!

Give new flavors of cold-pack cheese food a whirl in this hearty supper dish. Try sharp Cheddar with bacon, sharp Cheddar with garlic, sharp Cheddar with toasted onion, Cheddar with horseradish or even Swiss with roasted almonds!

1 Serving: Calories 700 (Calories from Fat 310); Total Fat 35g (Saturated Fat 19g; Trans Fat 1.5g); Cholesterol 145mg; Sodium 1760mg; Total Carbohydrate 56g (Dietary Fiber 6g; Sugars 8g); Protein 41g ✑ **% Daily Value:** Vitamin A 30%; Vitamin C 50%; Calcium 45%; Iron 30% ✑ **Exchanges:** 3 Starch, 1/2 Other Carbohydrate, 4 1/2 Medium-Fat Meat, 2 Fat ✑ **Carbohydrate Choices:** 4

Grilled Chili-Rubbed Pork Tenderloin

2 teaspoons packed brown sugar

1 1/2 teaspoons chili powder

1 teaspoon salt

1 teaspoon ground cumin

1/8 teaspoon ground red pepper
    (cayenne)

1 clove garlic, finely chopped

1 pork tenderloin (about 1 lb)

1 teaspoon vegetable oil

1 Heat gas or charcoal grill. In small bowl, mix all ingredients except pork and oil. Brush pork with oil. Rub and press spice mixture on all sides of pork.

2 Place pork on grill. Cover grill; cook over medium heat 17 to 20 minutes, turning several times, until pork has slight blush of pink in center and meat thermometer inserted in center reads 155°F. Cover pork; let stand about 5 minutes or until thermometer reads 160°F. Cut pork into slices.

4 servings

Easy Add-On

Imagine lively seasoned butter melting over this tender grilled pork! Just mix up a little extra of the seasoning rub mixture and stir it into softened butter. Pass it around to top the pork.

1 Serving: Calories 170 (Calories from Fat 50); Total Fat 6g (Saturated Fat 1.5g; Trans Fat 0g); Cholesterol 70mg; Sodium 650mg; Total Carbohydrate 3g (Dietary Fiber 0g; Sugars 2g); Protein 26g ✎ **% Daily Value:** Vitamin A 6%; Vitamin C 0%; Calcium 0%; Iron 10% ✎ **Exchanges:** 3 1/2 Very Lean Meat, 1 Fat ✎ **Carbohydrate Choices:** 0

Ginger-Peach Pork Medallions

1 tablespoon butter or margarine

1 pork tenderloin (1 lb), cut into 1/2-inch slices

1/4 teaspoon salt

1 large peach, peeled, sliced

2 tablespoons packed brown sugar

1 teaspoon grated gingerroot

2/3 cup chicken broth

2 teaspoons cornstarch

1 In 10-inch skillet, melt butter over medium-high heat. Sprinkle pork with salt; add to skillet. Cook about 4 minutes, turning pork once, until browned.

2 Stir in peach slices, brown sugar and gingerroot. Cook 2 minutes, stirring once or twice, until peach slices are tender.

3 In small bowl, mix broth and cornstarch; stir into pork and peach mixture. Reduce heat to medium-low. Cook 2 minutes, stirring once or twice, until thickened.

4 servings

Make it a Meal

The sweet and gingery flavor of this pork dish would go well with mashed sweet potatoes or seasoned sweet potato wedges or fries. Garnish the pork mixture with chopped fresh chives or parsley.

1 **Serving:** Calories 220 (Calories from Fat 70); Total Fat 8g (Saturated Fat 3.5g; Trans Fat 0g); Cholesterol 80mg; Sodium 390mg; Total Carbohydrate 12g (Dietary Fiber 0g; Sugars 10g); Protein 27g ✵ **% Daily Value:** Vitamin A 4%; Vitamin C 2%; Calcium 0%; Iron 10% ✵ **Exchanges:** 1/2 Other Carbohydrate, 4 Very Lean Meat, 1 Fat ✵ Carbohydrate Choices: 1

Prep Time **20 Minutes**
Start to Finish **20 Minutes**

Breaded Pork Chops

1/4 cup Original Bisquick mix

6 saltine cracker squares, crushed (1/4 cup)

1/2 teaspoon seasoned salt

1/8 teaspoon pepper

1 egg

1 tablespoon water

4 boneless pork loin chops, 1/2 inch thick (about 1 lb)

3 tablespoons vegetable oil

1 In shallow plate or dish, mix Bisquick mix, cracker crumbs, seasoned salt and pepper. In another shallow dish, mix egg and water.

2 Dip pork into egg mixture, then coat with Bisquick mixture.

3 In 10-inch nonstick skillet, heat oil over medium heat. Cook pork in oil 8 to 10 minutes, turning once, until no longer pink in center.

4 servings

Make it a Meal

These pork chops go perfectly with green beans and red potatoes. Dinner's ready!

1 Serving: Calories 330 (Calories from Fat 200); Total Fat 22g (Saturated Fat 5g; Trans Fat 0g); Cholesterol 125mg; Sodium 390mg; Total Carbohydrate 8g (Dietary Fiber 0g; Sugars 1g); Protein 27g **% Daily Value:** Vitamin A 0%; Vitamin C 0%; Calcium 4%; Iron 8% **Exchanges:** 1/2 Starch, 3 1/2 Lean Meat, 2 1/2 Fat **Carbohydrate Choices:** 1/2

Barbecue Pork Chops

1 1/2 cups barbecue-flavored potato chips (1 1/4 oz)

1/2 cup Original Bisquick mix

1 egg, beaten

2 tablespoons barbecue sauce

6 boneless pork loin chops, 1/2 inch thick (about 1 1/2 lb)

1 tablespoon vegetable oil

3/4 cup barbecue sauce

1 In 1-gallon resealable food-storage plastic bag, place potato chips; crush with rolling pin. Add Bisquick mix to chips; mix well.

2 In small shallow dish, mix egg and 2 tablespoons barbecue sauce. Dip pork chops into egg mixture, then shake in bag to coat with Bisquick mixture.

3 In 12-inch nonstick skillet, heat oil over medium-low heat. Cook pork chops in oil 15 to 18 minutes, turning once, until golden brown on outside and no longer pink in center. Serve with 3/4 cup barbecue sauce.

6 servings

Speed it Up

Tired of store-bought frozen food? Fill your freezer with these pork chops for a homemade meal anytime. If freezing, coat pork chops as directed, but don't cook them. Wrap each chop in heavy-duty foil; freeze up to 2 months. To thaw, place in refrigerator 8 hours or overnight. Cook as directed.

1 Serving: Calories 330 (Calories from Fat 140); Total Fat 15g (Saturated Fat 4.5g; Trans Fat 0g); Cholesterol 105mg; Sodium 600mg; Total Carbohydrate 23g (Dietary Fiber 0g; Sugars 11g); Protein 26g ❧ **% Daily Value:** Vitamin A 2%; Vitamin C 2%; Calcium 4%; Iron 10% ❧ **Exchanges:** 1 Starch, 1/2 Other Carbohydrate, 3 1/2 Lean Meat, 1 Fat ❧ **Carbohydrate Choices:** 1 1/2

Prep Time **20 Minutes**
Start to Finish **20 Minutes**

Grilled Mango Ham Steak

1 tablespoon packed brown sugar

1 tablespoon butter or margarine

Dash ground cloves

1 cup refrigerated sliced mango (from 1-lb 8-oz jar), cut into desired thickness

1 ham steak, 1/2 inch thick (about 1 1/4 lb)

1 lime, cut into wedges

1 Heat gas or charcoal grill. In 1-quart saucepan, cook brown sugar, butter, cloves and mango over medium heat about 5 minutes, stirring occasionally, until mango is hot. Remove from heat; cover to keep warm.

2 Place ham on grill. Cover grill; cook over medium heat 8 to 10 minutes, turning once, until thoroughly heated.

3 Spoon mango sauce over ham. Garnish with lime wedges.

4 servings

Instant **Success!**

Mango adds a tropical, sweet flavor that tastes great with salty ham. If fresh mangoes are in season, feel free to use them (see the tip on page 78 for cutting instructions). Papaya, peaches or nectarines are a good substitute.

1 Serving: Calories 320 (Calories from Fat 140); Total Fat 16g (Saturated Fat 6g; Trans Fat 0g); Cholesterol 90mg; Sodium 2150mg; Total Carbohydrate 12g (Dietary Fiber 1g; Sugars 9g); Protein 32g ✰ **% Daily Value:** Vitamin A 8%; Vitamin C 15%; Calcium 2%; Iron 10% ✰ **Exchanges:** 1/2 Fruit, 1/2 Other Carbohydrate, 4 1/2 Lean Meat, 1/2 Fat ✰ **Carbohydrate Choices:** 1

Betty Crocker quick & easy cookbook

Prep Time **20 Minutes**
Start to Finish **20 Minutes**

Grilled Maple-Mustard Ham Steak

1/3 cup maple-flavored syrup

1 tablespoon yellow mustard

2 medium green onions, sliced (2 tablespoons)

1 ham steak, 1/2 inch thick (about 1 1/4 lb)

1 Heat gas or charcoal grill. In small bowl, mix syrup, mustard and onions. Reserve 3 tablespoons syrup mixture in separate small microwavable bowl. Brush remaining mixture on ham.

2 Place ham on grill. Cover grill; cook over medium heat 8 to 10 minutes, turning once, until browned. Microwave reserved syrup mixture uncovered on High 20 to 30 seconds or until hot. Place ham on serving platter; pour syrup mixture over ham.

4 servings

Instant Success!

Ham steaks, also called ham slices, are a terrific item to keep on hand for quick meals. They don't need to be gussied up, but this maple syrup and mustard glaze with a little hit of onion really hits the spot.

1 Serving: Calories 290 (Calories from Fat 100); Total Fat 11g (Saturated Fat 4g; Trans Fat 0g); Cholesterol 70mg; Sodium 1880mg; Total Carbohydrate 21g (Dietary Fiber 0g; Sugars 10g); Protein 27g ✤ **% Daily Value:** Vitamin A 0%; Vitamin C 0%; Calcium 0%; Iron 10% ✤ **Exchanges:** 1 1/2 Other Carbohydrate, 4 Lean Meat ✤ **Carbohydrate Choices:** 1 1/2

fish & seafood

Add Dessert

A dish of ice cream can satisfy, but for nearly effortless "oohs and aahs," express yourself in a new way. Here's how.

1 **Brownie Volcanoes:** Cut brownies into 1- to 1 1/2-inch squares and mound in individual shallow serving bowls to resemble a volcano. Drizzle with ice cream toppings, and top with whipped topping and a cherry.

2 **Double-Chocolate Truffles:** Drizzle warm hot fudge topping in a zigzag pattern on very small individual serving plates; place a purchased truffle in the center of the plate. Garnish with a few fresh raspberries or slices of strawberry if desired, or dust very, very lightly with unsweetened baking cocoa or powdered sugar.

3 **Puddin' Parfaits:** Alternate layers of purchased ready-to-eat pudding with crushed cookie crumbs and whipped topping. Top with gummy worms for extra fun.

4 **Yogurt, Fruit and Granola Parfaits:** Alternate layers of yogurt with fresh or canned fruit and granola or crushed cereal.

5 **Elegant Orange-Kiwifruit:** On a serving platter or individual serving plates, arrange sliced oranges and kiwifruit; drizzle with warm caramel or chocolate topping, and sprinkle with toasted sliced almonds.

6 **Heavenly Angel Food:** Make a box of regular (not instant) vanilla pudding with half-and-half or whipping cream instead of milk. Serve warm over purchased angel food cake slices; garnish with fresh fruit if desired.

7 **Caramel Apple Pie with Toasted Pecans:** Serve warm slices of purchased apple pie with warmed caramel topping and toasted pecan halves. Add vanilla or cinnamon ice cream if you must! If you're baking a frozen pie or warming a prebaked pie, toast the pecans at the same time; they take about 6 to 10 minutes.

8 **Sorbet Trio:** Purchase three different kinds of sorbet, like mango, raspberry and lemon. Place scoop of each flavor in small individual serving bowls; serve with fancy store-bought cookies like pirouettes.

9 **Paradise Pineapple:** In a shallow baking dish, arrange fresh or canned pineapple slices (look for peeled and cored whole fresh pineapple in the produce aisle); pat dry with paper towels. Sprinkle with brown sugar and a little cinnamon. Broil with tops 4 to 6 inches from heat just until brown sugar becomes bubbly. Sprinkle with coconut. Serve with whipped cream or vanilla ice cream if desired.

10 **Lemon Shortcake Cups:** Mix equal amounts of whipped topping or whipped cream with canned lemon pie filling; spoon into purchased sponge-type shortcake cups. Top with fresh blueberries.

This icon means: 20 minutes or less

Basil Salmon and Julienne Vegetables

1 tablespoon butter or margarine

1 bag (1 lb) frozen bell pepper and onion stir-fry

1 medium zucchini, cut into julienne (matchstick-size) strips

1 1/2 lb salmon fillets, about 1/2 inch thick, cut into 4 serving pieces

2 tablespoons chopped fresh basil leaves

1/2 teaspoon seasoned salt

1 teaspoon lemon-pepper seasoning

1/4 cup chicken broth

1 In 12-inch nonstick skillet, melt butter over medium heat. Add bell pepper mixture. Cook and stir 2 minutes. Stir in zucchini.

2 Place fish, skin side down, in skillet, pushing down into vegetables if necessary. Sprinkle fish and vegetables with basil, seasoned salt and lemon-pepper seasoning. Pour broth over fish and vegetables.

3 Cover; cook over medium-low heat 8 to 10 minutes or until fish flakes easily with fork. Remove fish and vegetables from skillet with slotted spoon.

4 servings

Instant **Success!**

Make short work of cutting up the zucchini with this technique. Cut the whole "zuke" crosswise into 2- to 3-inch sections. Then, stand a section on its end and cut it from top to bottom into 1/8-inch slices. Next, lay the slices flat, stack them, and cut the stack lengthwise into 1/8-inch match-like sticks.

1 Serving: Calories 320 (Calories from Fat 120); Total Fat 13g (Saturated Fat 4.5g; Trans Fat 0g); Cholesterol 120mg; Sodium 450mg; Total Carbohydrate 12g (Dietary Fiber 2g; Sugars 5g); Protein 38g ✌ **% Daily Value:** Vitamin A 10%; Vitamin C 50%; Calcium 4%; Iron 10% ✌ **Exchanges:** 1/2 Other Carbohydrate, 1 Vegetable, 5 Lean Meat ✌ Carbohydrate Choices: 1

Betty Crocker quick & easy cookbook

Baked Salmon
with Cilantro

Prep Time **5 Minutes**
Start to Finish **25 Minutes**

Cooking spray

1/4 cup butter or margarine,
    slightly softened

1 tablespoon chopped fresh cilantro

1/2 teaspoon grated lemon peel

1 1/2 lb salmon, red snapper or other
    medium-firm fish fillets, about 1 inch
    thick, cut into 4 serving pieces

1/4 teaspoon salt

1/4 teaspoon ground cumin

1 tablespoon lemon juice

1   Heat oven to 425°F. Line 13 × 9-inch pan with foil; spray foil with cooking spray. In small bowl, mix butter, cilantro and lemon peel. Cover butter; refrigerate while preparing fish.

2   Place fish, skin side down, in pan. Sprinkle with salt and cumin. Drizzle with lemon juice.

3   Bake 15 to 20 minutes or until fish flakes easily with fork. Carefully lift fish from skin with pancake turner. Top each serving of fish with butter mixture.

4 servings

Make it a Meal

Having people over? The recipe is easy to double. Serve the salmon on a bed of angel hair pasta or skin-on mashed potatoes (look for the new refrigerated ready-to-eat varieties) on a pretty serving platter. Garnish the platter with cilantro sprigs and slices of lemon.

1 Serving: Calories 340 (Calories from Fat 190); Total Fat 21g (Saturated Fat 10g; Trans Fat 0.5g); Cholesterol 140mg; Sodium 330mg; Total Carbohydrate 0g (Dietary Fiber 0g; Sugars 0g); Protein 36g ✧ **% Daily Value:** Vitamin A 10%; Vitamin C 4%; Calcium 2%; Iron 6% ✧ **Exchanges:** 5 Lean Meat, 1 1/2 Fat ✧ **Carbohydrate Choices:** 0

Grilled Salmon with Nectarine Salsa

2 lb salmon fillets, about 1/2 inch thick,
    cut into 6 serving pieces

1/2 cup lemon juice

4 medium nectarines or peaches, chopped

1/2 cup chopped fresh cilantro

2 teaspoons chopped jalapeño chile

1 Heat gas or charcoal grill.

2 Place fish, skin side down, on grill; drizzle with 1/4 cup lemon juice Cover grill; cook over medium heat 10 to 20 minutes or until fish flakes easily with fork.

3 In medium bowl, mix remaining ingredients and remaining 1/4 cup lemon juice. Serve nectarine salsa over fish.

6 servings

Make it a Meal

An easy spinach salad goes perfectly with this sweet 'n succulent dish. Just open a bag of washed fresh baby spinach leaves, toss in some raisins, sliced mushrooms and maybe a few chopped nuts, and voilà!

1 Serving: Calories 260 (Calories from Fat 80); Total Fat 9g (Saturated Fat 2.5g; Trans Fat 0g); Cholesterol 100mg; Sodium 95mg; Total Carbohydrate 11g (Dietary Fiber 2g; Sugars 8g); Protein 33g ✎ **% Daily Value:** Vitamin A 10%; Vitamin C 20%; Calcium 2%; Iron 8% ✎ **Exchanges:** 1/2 Fruit, 4 1/2 Lean Meat ✎ **Carbohydrate Choices:** 1

Prep Time **30 Minutes**
Start to Finish **30 Minutes**

Grilled Maple-Dijon Salmon and Asparagus Salad

DRESSING

1/3 cup maple-flavored syrup

2 tablespoons Dijon mustard

2 tablespoons olive or vegetable oil

SALAD

1 lb asparagus spears

1 1/2 lb salmon fillets, about 1/2 inch thick, cut into 4 serving pieces

4 cups fresh baby salad greens

1 cup shredded carrots (about 2 medium)

2 hard-cooked eggs, cut into 8 wedges

Freshly ground pepper, if desired

1 Heat gas or charcoal grill. In small bowl, mix all dressing ingredients with wire whisk.

2 Break off tough ends of asparagus as far down as stalks snap easily. Brush fish with 1 tablespoon of the dressing. In 11 × 7-inch glass baking dish, toss asparagus and 1 tablespoon of the dressing. Place asparagus in grill basket (grill "wok").

3 Place grill basket and fish, skin side down, on grill. Cover grill; cook asparagus over medium heat 7 to 10 minutes, shaking grill basket or turning asparagus occasionally, until crisp-tender; cook fish 10 to 15 minutes or until fish flakes easily with fork.

4 Slide pancake turner between fish and skin to remove each piece from skin. Among 4 plates, divide salad greens, carrots and eggs. Top with fish and asparagus. Sprinkle with pepper. Serve with remaining dressing.

4 servings

Instant Success!

Too hot for a hot salad? Try it cold. Grill the salmon and asparagus, cook the eggs and make the dressing up to one day ahead of time. Cover and refrigerate until serving.

1 Serving: Calories 420 (Calories from Fat 170); Total Fat 19g (Saturated Fat 4g; Trans Fat 0g); Cholesterol 200mg; Sodium 370mg; Total Carbohydrate 27g (Dietary Fiber 3g; Sugars 13g); Protein 37g ❧ **% Daily Value:** Vitamin A 140%; Vitamin C 20%; Calcium 8%; Iron 15% ❧ **Exchanges:** 1 Other Carbohydrate, 2 Vegetable, 4 1/2 Lean Meat, 1 Fat ❧ **Carbohydrate Choices:** 2

Betty Crocker quick & easy cookbook

Orange and Dill Pan-Seared Tuna

Prep Time **20 Minutes**
Start to Finish **20 Minutes**

1 tablespoon butter or margarine

1 tablespoon olive or vegetable oil

1 1/2 lb tuna, swordfish or other firm
    fish steaks, about 3/4 inch thick,
    cut into 4 serving pieces

1 teaspoon peppered seasoned salt

1/2 cup thinly sliced red onion

3/4 cup orange juice

1 tablespoon chopped fresh or
    1/4 teaspoon dried dill weed

1 tablespoon butter or margarine

1 teaspoon grated orange peel,
    if desired

1 In 10-inch nonstick skillet, heat 1 tablespoon butter and the oil over medium-high heat. Sprinkle both sides of fish with peppered seasoned salt. Add fish to skillet; cook about 1 minute on each side until golden brown. Reduce heat to medium-low. Cook 3 to 4 minutes longer, turning once, until fish flakes easily with fork (tuna steaks will also be slightly pink in center). Remove fish from skillet; keep warm.

2 Add onion to skillet. Cook over medium heat 2 minutes, stirring occasionally. Stir in orange juice; cook 2 minutes. Stir in dill weed, 1 tablespoon butter and the orange peel. Cook 1 to 2 minutes or until slightly thickened. Serve sauce over fish.

4 servings

Make it a Meal

Fresh green beans or asparagus and lightly buttered new potatoes pair well with this citrus-flavored fish. For a stylish, easy garnish, use orange slices and dill sprigs.

1 Serving: Calories 320 (Calories from Fat 160); Total Fat 18g (Saturated Fat 7g; Trans Fat 0g); Cholesterol 115mg; Sodium 480mg; Total Carbohydrate 7g (Dietary Fiber 0g; Sugars 6g); Protein 33g ❧ **% Daily Value:** Vitamin A 8%; Vitamin C 20%; Calcium 2%; Iron 6% ❧ **Exchanges:** 1/2 Other Carbohydrate, 4 1/2 Very Lean Meat, 3 Fat ❧ **Carbohydrate Choices:** 1/2

Grilled Teriyaki Tuna Salad

DRESSING

1/2 cup pineapple juice

1/4 cup teriyaki baste and glaze
(from 12-oz bottle)

1 tablespoon sesame oil

1/4 teaspoon ground ginger

SALAD

12 pieces (1 1/2 inches each) fresh
pineapple (2 cups)

1 1/2 lb tuna steaks, about 3/4 inch thick,
cut into 4 serving pieces

4 cups bite-size pieces mixed salad greens

1 cup grape or cherry tomatoes, cut in half

1 small red onion, sliced and separated
into rings

1/2 cup sesame oat bran sticks or croutons

1 Spray grill rack with cooking spray. Heat gas or charcoal grill. In small bowl, mix all dressing ingredients with wire whisk; reserve 2 tablespoons.

2 On each of 2 (10-inch) metal skewers, thread pineapple, leaving 1/4-inch space between each piece. Brush 1 tablespoon of the reserved dressing on pineapple; brush remaining 1 tablespoon reserved dressing on fish.

3 Place fish on grill. Cover grill; cook over medium heat about 10 minutes, turning once and adding pineapple for last 5 minutes of grilling, until fish flakes easily with fork.

4 Among 4 plates, divide salad greens, tomatoes and onion. Top with pineapple and tuna. Sprinkle with sesame sticks. Serve with remaining dressing.

4 servings

Instant **Success!**

Keeping a few bastes in your pantry lets you grill at a moment's notice. One of the most versatile is teriyaki baste and glaze; it has a thick, syruplike consistency and shouldn't be confused with teriyaki marinade or sauce, which is more watery. If you like, use stir-fry sauce instead, but look for a thicker brand.

1 Serving: Calories 420 (Calories from Fat 140); Total Fat 15g (Saturated Fat 3.5g; Trans Fat 0g); Cholesterol 100mg; Sodium 710mg; Total Carbohydrate 35g (Dietary Fiber 4g; Sugars 18g); Protein 36g ✃ **% Daily Value:** Vitamin A 70%; Vitamin C 80%; Calcium 8%; Iron 15% ✃ **Exchanges:** 1/2 Starch, 1 Fruit, 1/2 Other Carbohydrate, 1 Vegetable, 4 1/2 Very Lean Meat, 2 1/2 Fat ✃ **Carbohydrate Choices:** 2

Grilled Lemon-Garlic Halibut Steaks

1/4 cup lemon juice

1 tablespoon olive or vegetable oil

1/4 teaspoon salt

1/4 teaspoon pepper

2 cloves garlic, finely chopped

2 lb halibut or tuna steaks, about 3/4 inch thick, cut into 4 serving pieces

1/4 cup chopped fresh parsley

1 tablespoon grated lemon peel

1 Brush grill rack with vegetable oil. Heat gas or charcoal grill. In shallow glass or plastic dish or resealable food-storage plastic bag, mix lemon juice, oil, salt, pepper and garlic. Add fish; turn several times to coat. Cover dish or seal bag; refrigerate 10 minutes to marinate.

2 Remove fish from marinade; reserve marinade. Place fish on grill. Cover grill; cook over medium heat 10 to 15 minutes, turning once and brushing with marinade, until fish flakes easily with fork (tuna steaks will also be slightly pink in center). Discard any remaining marinade.

3 Sprinkle fish with parsley and lemon peel.

4 servings

Make it a Meal

Light and easy is the name of the game here. If you have a grill basket (grill "wok"), grill some snow peas for a crisp refreshing side. Or cook them till crisp-tender in boiling water.

1 Serving: Calories 240 (Calories from Fat 60); Total Fat 6g (Saturated Fat 1g; Trans Fat 0g); Cholesterol 120mg; Sodium 340mg; Total Carbohydrate 2g (Dietary Fiber 0g; Sugars 0g); Protein 43g ✎ **% Daily Value:** Vitamin A 8%; Vitamin C 10%; Calcium 4%; Iron 6% ✎ **Exchanges:** 6 Very Lean Meat, 1/2 Fat ✎ **Carbohydrate Choices:** 0

Grilled Latin Halibut with Green Sauce

2 1/2 lb halibut or sea bass steaks, about 3/4 inch thick, cut into 6 serving pieces

1 tablespoon olive or vegetable oil

1 teaspoon seasoned salt

1 jar (16 oz) green salsa (salsa verde) (2 cups)

1 ripe avocado, pitted, peeled and chopped

2 tablespoons chopped ripe olives

Sour cream, if desired

Fresh cilantro leaves, if desired

1 Heat gas or charcoal grill. Brush fish lightly with oil; sprinkle with seasoned salt.

2 Place fish on grill. Cover grill; cook over medium-high heat about 10 minutes, turning once, until fish flakes easily with fork.

3 In medium bowl, mix salsa, avocado and olives. Serve over fish. Garnish with sour cream and cilantro.

6 servings

Instant **Success!**

Even though green salsa is becoming more mainstream, tomato salsa is readily available and a wonderful alternative. Add olives and fresh avocados to the salsa for extra flair.

1 Serving: Calories 270 (Calories from Fat 90); Total Fat 10g (Saturated Fat 1.5g; Trans Fat 0g); Cholesterol 100mg; Sodium 480mg; Total Carbohydrate 8g (Dietary Fiber 3g; Sugars 3g); Protein 37g ✍ **% Daily Value:** Vitamin A 8%; Vitamin C 45%; Calcium 4%; Iron 8% ✍ **Exchanges:** 1/2 Other Carbohydrate, 5 Very Lean Meat, 1 1/2 Fat ✍ **Carbohydrate Choices:** 1/2

Gremolata-Topped Sea Bass

Prep Time **5 Minutes**
Start to Finish **25 Minutes**

Cooking spray

1/4 cup Italian-style dry bread crumbs

1/4 cup chopped fresh parsley

2 teaspoons grated lemon peel

1 tablespoon butter or margarine, melted

1 lb sea bass, mahi-mahi or other medium-firm fish fillets, cut into 4 serving pieces

1/4 teaspoon seasoned salt

1 tablespoon lemon juice

1 Heat oven to 425°F. Line 13 × 9-inch pan with foil; spray foil with cooking spray. In small bowl, mix bread crumbs, parsley, lemon peel and butter.

2 Place fish in pan. Sprinkle with seasoned salt. Drizzle with lemon juice. Spoon crumb mixture over each piece; press lightly.

3 Bake 15 to 20 minutes or until fish flakes easily with fork.

4 servings

Instant
Success!

It almost takes less time to assemble than it takes to say "gremolata." This zesty citrus-flavored breading also makes a great topping for broiled lamb chops.

1 Serving: Calories 180 (Calories from Fat 70); Total Fat 8g (Saturated Fat 3g; Trans Fat 0g); Cholesterol 65mg; Sodium 290mg; Total Carbohydrate 6g (Dietary Fiber 0g; Sugars 0g); Protein 23g ❧ **% Daily Value:** Vitamin A 10%; Vitamin C 6%; Calcium 4%; Iron 10% ❧ **Exchanges:** 1/2 Starch, 3 Very Lean Meat, 1 Fat ❧ **Carbohydrate Choices:** 1/2

Brown Butter Fish Florentine

1/4 cup all-purpose flour

1 lb tilapia fillets, about 1/2 inch thick, cut into 4 serving pieces

1/2 teaspoon salt

1 teaspoon lemon-pepper seasoning

1/4 cup butter*

1 bag (9 oz) washed fresh baby spinach leaves

1/2 red bell pepper, cut into thin slivers

1/4 cup slivered almonds, toasted**

1 In shallow dish, place flour. Sprinkle fish with salt and lemon-pepper seasoning; dip in flour to coat.

2 In 12-inch nonstick skillet, heat butter over medium heat 3 to 4 minutes, stirring constantly, until light golden brown. Add fish. Cook 6 to 8 minutes, turning once, until outside is browned and fish flakes easily with fork. Remove to plate; cover to keep warm.

3 Add spinach and bell pepper to butter in skillet. Cook 2 to 4 minutes, stirring frequently, until tender. On 4 dinner plates, spoon spinach mixture; top with fish. Sprinkle with almonds.

4 servings

Do not use margarine or spreads.

**To toast nuts, bake uncovered in ungreased shallow pan in 350°F oven 6 to 10 minutes, stirring occasionally, until light brown. Or cook in ungreased heavy skillet over medium heat 5 to 7 minutes, stirring frequently until browning begins, then stirring constantly until golden brown.*

Make it a Meal

Superb, elegant and extremely simple! The browned butter flavor will knock your socks off. You don't want to waste even a tiny drop of the butter, so serve the fish and vegetables over angel hair pasta to soak it up.

1 Serving: Calories 300 (Calories from Fat 150); Total Fat 17g (Saturated Fat 8g; Trans Fat 0.5g); Cholesterol 90mg; Sodium 610mg; Total Carbohydrate 11g (Dietary Fiber 3g; Sugars 1g); Protein 26g ✑ **% Daily Value:** Vitamin A 140%; Vitamin C 40%; Calcium 10%; Iron 15% ✑ **Exchanges:** 1/2 Starch, 1 Vegetable, 3 Lean Meat, 1 1/2 Fat ✑ **Carbohydrate Choices:** 1

Crispy Herbed Fish Fillets

1 lb flounder fillets, about 1/2 inch thick,
    cut into 4 serving pieces

2 eggs

1 1/4 cups panko bread crumbs

1 teaspoon grated lemon peel

1 teaspoon dried marjoram leaves

1/2 teaspoon salt

1/4 teaspoon pepper

1/4 cup olive or vegetable oil

1   Dry fish well on paper towels. In shallow dish, beat eggs with fork or wire whisk until well mixed. In another shallow dish, mix bread crumbs, lemon peel, marjoram, salt and pepper.

2   In 12-inch nonstick skillet, heat 2 tablespoons of the oil over medium heat. Dip fish in eggs, then coat well with crumb mixture. Add about half of the fish in single layer to oil. Cook 3 to 4 minutes, carefully turning once, until outside is browned and crisp and fish flakes easily with fork.

3   Remove cooked fish to plate; cover to keep warm. Repeat with remaining oil and fish.

4 servings

Instant
Success!

Panko, or Japanese bread crumbs, are coarse in texture. Once you try panko, you'll be hooked—they're crunchier and make a more attractive coating!

1 **Serving:** Calories 310 (Calories from Fat 160); Total Fat 17g (Saturated Fat 3g; Trans Fat 0g); Cholesterol 160mg; Sodium 440mg; Total Carbohydrate 14g (Dietary Fiber 0g; Sugars 0g); Protein 25g ✍ **% Daily Value:** Vitamin A 4%; Vitamin C 0%; Calcium 4%; Iron 6% ✍ **Exchanges:** 1 Starch, 3 Very Lean Meat, 3 Fat ✍ **Carbohydrate Choices:** 1

Betty Crocker quick & easy cookbook

Lemony Fish over Vegetables and Rice

1 box (6 oz) fried rice (rice and vermicelli mix with almonds and Oriental seasonings)

2 tablespoons butter or margarine

2 cups water

1/2 teaspoon grated lemon peel

1 bag (1 lb) frozen broccoli, corn and peppers (or other combination)

1 lb cod, haddock or other mild-flavored fish fillets, about 1/2 inch thick, cut into 4 serving pieces

1/2 teaspoon lemon-pepper seasoning

1 tablespoon lemon juice

Chopped fresh parsley, if desired

1 In 12-inch nonstick skillet, cook rice and butter over medium heat about 3 minutes, stirring occasionally, until rice is golden brown. Stir in water, seasoning packet from rice mix and lemon peel. Heat to boiling; reduce heat to low. Cover; simmer 10 minutes.

2 Stir in frozen vegetables. Heat to boiling over medium-high heat, stirring occasionally. Arrange fish on rice mixture. Sprinkle fish with lemon-pepper seasoning; drizzle with lemon juice.

3 Reduce heat to low. Cover; simmer 8 to 12 minutes or until fish flakes easily with fork and vegetables are tender. Sprinkle with parsley.

4 servings

Make it a Meal

What could be easier than making a meal in one skillet? (Well, maybe pizza delivery.) Add a salad kit or bagged greens and your favorite dressing and dinner is a go!

1 Serving: Calories 250 (Calories from Fat 70); Total Fat 8g (Saturated Fat 4g; Trans Fat 0g); Cholesterol 75mg; Sodium 620mg; Total Carbohydrate 19g (Dietary Fiber 3g; Sugars 2g); Protein 26g ✌ **% Daily Value:** Vitamin A 25%; Vitamin C 35%; Calcium 6%; Iron 10% ✌ **Exchanges:** 1 Starch, 1 Vegetable, 3 Very Lean Meat, 1 Fat ✌ **Carbohydrate Choices:** 1

Marinara Shrimp and Vegetable Bowls

8 oz uncooked vermicelli

1 tablespoon olive or vegetable oil

2 cloves garlic, finely chopped

1/2 cup red onion wedges

1 medium zucchini, cut into 2 × 1/4-inch strips

1 medium yellow summer squash, cut into 2 × 1/4-inch strips

1/4 teaspoon salt

1 lb uncooked deveined peeled medium or large shrimp, thawed if frozen, tail shells removed

1 cup marinara sauce

2 tablespoons chopped fresh or 1/2 teaspoon dried basil leaves

1 Cook and drain vermicelli as directed on package. Meanwhile, in 10-inch skillet, heat oil over medium heat. Cook garlic and onion in oil 2 to 3 minutes, stirring frequently, until onion is crisp-tender. Stir in zucchini, yellow squash and salt. Cook 2 to 3 minutes, stirring frequently, just until squash is tender; remove vegetables from skillet.

2 Add shrimp to skillet. Cook over medium heat 1 to 2 minutes, stirring frequently, until shrimp are pink. Meanwhile, in 1-quart saucepan, heat marinara sauce over medium heat, stirring occasionally, until hot.

3 Among 4 bowls, divide vermicelli; toss each serving with about 2 tablespoons marinara sauce. Top with vegetables and shrimp. Drizzle with remaining marinara sauce. Sprinkle with basil.

4 servings

Speed it Up

Here's a recipe where dovetailing—that is, making several parts of the recipe at once—saves loads of time. While the pasta water comes to a boil, start chopping the veggies. Then while the pasta cooks, start the shrimp and heat the marinara sauce. Dinner will be ready 1-2-3!

1 Serving: Calories 430 (Calories from Fat 70); Total Fat 8g (Saturated Fat 1g; Trans Fat 0g); Cholesterol 160mg; Sodium 880mg; Total Carbohydrate 63g (Dietary Fiber 6g; Sugars 9g); Protein 27g ✌ **% Daily Value:** Vitamin A 15%; Vitamin C 20%; Calcium 8%; Iron 35% ✌ **Exchanges:** 3 1/2 Starch, 1/2 Other Carbohydrate, 1 Vegetable, 2 Very Lean Meat, 1 Fat ✌ **Carbohydrate Choices:** 4

Betty Crocker quick & easy cookbook

Scampi with Fettuccine

8 oz uncooked fettuccine

2 tablespoons olive or vegetable oil

1 1/2 lb uncooked deveined peeled
medium shrimp, thawed if frozen,
tail shells removed

2 medium green onions, thinly sliced
(2 tablespoons)

2 cloves garlic, finely chopped

1 tablespoon chopped fresh or
1/2 teaspoon dried basil leaves

1 tablespoon chopped fresh parsley

2 tablespoons lemon juice

1/4 teaspoon salt

1 Cook and drain fettuccine as directed on package. Meanwhile, in 10-inch skillet, heat oil over medium heat. Cook remaining ingredients in oil 2 to 3 minutes, stirring frequently, until shrimp are pink; remove from heat.

2 Toss fettuccine with shrimp mixture in skillet.

4 servings

Speed it Up

Peeling and deveining shrimp is time consuming—and unnecessary! Luckily for us, somebody else has done this laborious task. Look for fresh or frozen shrimp that has already been peeled and deveined.

1 Serving: Calories 380 (Calories from Fat 90); Total Fat 10g (Saturated Fat 1.5g; Trans Fat 0g); Cholesterol 290mg; Sodium 670mg; Total Carbohydrate 38g (Dietary Fiber 2g; Sugars 0g); Protein 33g ✿ **% Daily Value:** Vitamin A 10%; Vitamin C 6%; Calcium 8%; Iron 35% ✿ **Exchanges:** 2 1/2 Starch, 3 1/2 Very Lean Meat, 1 1/2 Fat ✿ **Carbohydrate Choices:** 2 1/2

Caesar Shrimp Salad

Prep Time **25 Minutes**
Start to Finish **25 Minutes**

4 cups uncooked medium pasta shells (10 oz)

1 cup shredded Parmesan cheese (4 oz)

1 cup reduced-fat creamy Caesar dressing

8 medium green onions, sliced (1/2 cup)

1 1/2 lb frozen cooked deveined peeled shrimp, thawed, drained and tail shells removed

1 bag (10 oz) ready-to-eat romaine lettuce (7 cups)

2 cups Caesar-flavored croutons

1 Cook and drain pasta as directed on package. Rinse with cold water; drain.

2 In very large (4-quart) bowl, place pasta, cheese, dressing, onions and shrimp; toss. Just before serving, add lettuce and croutons; toss.

8 servings (2 cups each)

Make it a Meal

Crisp breadsticks are perfect with this salad. The cracker aisle usually has plain and flavored versions that are either long and skinny or shorter and a bit wider.

1 Serving: Calories 370 (Calories from Fat 80); Total Fat 9g (Saturated Fat 3.5g; Trans Fat 0.5g); Cholesterol 180mg; Sodium 1000mg; Total Carbohydrate 42g (Dietary Fiber 4g; Sugars 5g); Protein 30g ❧ **% Daily Value:** Vitamin A 60%; Vitamin C 25%; Calcium 25%; Iron 30% ❧ **Exchanges:** 2 Starch, 1/2 Other Carbohydrate, 1 Vegetable, 3 Very Lean Meat, 1 Fat ❧ **Carbohydrate Choices:** 3

Prep Time **20 Minutes**
Start to Finish **20 Minutes**

Grilled Herbed Seafood

8 oz uncooked thin spaghetti or vermicelli

Cooking spray

1/2 lb bay scallops

1/2 lb orange roughy fillets, cut into 1-inch pieces

1/2 lb uncooked deveined peeled large shrimp, thawed if frozen, tail shells removed

2 tablespoons chopped fresh or 2 teaspoons dried marjoram leaves

1/2 teaspoon grated lemon peel

1/8 teaspoon white pepper

3 tablespoons butter or margarine, melted

2 tablespoons lemon juice

1 Heat gas or charcoal grill. Cook and drain spaghetti as directed on package.

2 Meanwhile, cut 18-inch square of heavy-duty foil; spray with cooking spray. On center of foil square, arrange scallops, fish and shrimp, placing shrimp on top. Sprinkle with marjoram, lemon peel and white pepper. Drizzle with butter and lemon juice. Bring corners of foil up to center and seal loosely.

3 Place packet on grill. Cover grill; cook over medium heat 8 to 10 minutes, rotating packet 1/2 turn after 5 minutes, until scallops are white, fish flakes easily with fork and shrimp are pink. Serve seafood mixture over spaghetti.

4 servings

Instant
Success!

Using foil packets on the grill is the no-hassle (and no clean-up) way to go! Just open, eat and toss the foil. Bay scallops are sweeter and more tender and succulent than the larger sea scallops. If you use sea scallops, cut each in half.

1 Serving: Calories 420 (Calories from Fat 100); Total Fat 11g (Saturated Fat 6g; Trans Fat 0.5g); Cholesterol 150mg; Sodium 510mg; Total Carbohydrate 46g (Dietary Fiber 3g; Sugars 0g); Protein 34g ✌ **% Daily Value:** Vitamin A 8%; Vitamin C 2%; Calcium 8%; Iron 25% ✌ **Exchanges:** 3 Starch, 3 1/2 Very Lean Meat, 1 1/2 Fat ✌ **Carbohydrate Choices:** 3

Betty Crocker quick & easy cookbook

Seafood Rice Skillet

1 tablespoon olive or vegetable oil

1 medium onion, chopped (1/2 cup)

1 can (14 oz) chicken broth

1 cup uncooked medium or long-grain white rice

1 cup ready-to-eat baby-cut carrots, cut in half lengthwise

1/2 cup water

1/2 teaspoon garlic-pepper blend

2 cups washed fresh baby spinach leaves

1 package (8 oz) refrigerated imitation crabmeat chunks

1/4 cup shredded Parmesan cheese (1 oz)

1 In 12-inch nonstick skillet, heat oil over medium-high heat. Cook onion in oil 2 to 3 minutes, stirring occasionally, until crisp-tender. Stir in broth; heat to boiling. Stir in rice; reduce heat. Cover; simmer 10 minutes without stirring.

2 Stir in carrots, water and garlic-pepper blend. Cover; simmer 8 to 10 minutes without stirring until rice is tender.

3 Stir in spinach until wilted. Stir in imitation crabmeat and cheese.

4 servings

Instant
Success!

Cooking rice in chicken broth instead of water gives it lots of extra flavor without adding extra time or effort; in fact, "chicken rice" is a great alternative to white rice anytime. And the trick works for other starches, too, like couscous.

1 Serving: Calories 340 (Calories from Fat 60); Total Fat 7g (Saturated Fat 2g; Trans Fat 0g); Cholesterol 25mg; Sodium 1060mg; Total Carbohydrate 50g (Dietary Fiber 2g; Sugars 2g); Protein 18g ❧ **% Daily Value:** Vitamin A 100%; Vitamin C 6%; Calcium 15%; Iron 15% ❧ **Exchanges:** 3 Starch, 1 Vegetable, 1 Very Lean Meat, 1 Fat ❧ **Carbohydrate Choices:** 3

Prep Time **15 Minutes**
Start to Finish **15 Minutes**

Apple-Fennel Lobster Salad

2 packages (6 oz each) refrigerated
    salad-style imitation lobster

1 red apple, halved, cored and thinly
    sliced (1 cup)

1 fennel bulb, cut in half, thinly sliced
    (1 1/4 cups)

1/4 cup golden raisins

1/3 cup mayonnaise or salad dressing

1/2 teaspoon salt

1/2 teaspoon ground mustard

2 tablespoons frozen apple juice
    concentrate, thawed, or apple juice

4 cups torn romaine lettuce

1/2 cup chopped walnuts, if desired

1 In medium bowl, mix imitation lobster, apple, fennel and raisins.

2 In small bowl, beat mayonnaise, salt, mustard and apple juice concentrate
with wire whisk until well blended. Pour over lobster mixture; toss.

3 Among 4 plates, divide lettuce. Top with lobster salad. Sprinkle with
walnuts.

4 servings

Instant **Success!**

*Like them tart or sweet, crisp
or soft? It doesn't matter; just
use your favorite apple in this
upscale, bistro-style salad.
Reserve the frilly fronds of
the fennel bulb for a very
pretty garnish.*

1 Serving: Calories 300 (Calories from Fat 140); Total Fat 16g (Saturated Fat 2.5g; Trans Fat 0g); Cholesterol 30mg;
Sodium 1160mg; Total Carbohydrate 25g (Dietary Fiber 3g; Sugars 13g); Protein 15g ✼ **% Daily Value:** Vitamin A 70%;
Vitamin C 30%; Calcium 6%; Iron 8% ✼ **Exchanges:** 1 Other Carbohydrate, 1 Vegetable, 2 Very Lean Meat, 3 Fat ✼
Carbohydrate Choices: 1 1/2

5 pasta & pizza

Salads on the Side

Go beyond a bag of lettuce or a complete salad mix with one of these simple taste sensations!

1 **Hearts of Palm:** Drain and slice canned or jarred hearts of palm; drizzle with your favorite vinaigrette dressing.

2 **Cukes and Tomatoes:** On a serving platter or individual salad plates, arrange cucumber chunks or slices with tomato wedges or slices. Sprinkle with salt and pepper; drizzle with your favorite dressing or add a splash of vinegar.

3 **Mediterranean Vegetable Salad:** On a serving platter, arrange sliced tomatoes and sliced bell peppers; drizzle with your favorite vinaigrette dressing. Top with pitted kalamata olives or small whole pitted ripe olives; sprinkle with crumbled feta cheese.

4 **Artichokes and Greens:** Toss prewashed bagged salad greens, jarred marinated artichoke hearts (undrained) and Caesar-flavored croutons.

5 **Cheddar, Bacon and Smoked Almond Salad:** Toss prewashed bagged salad greens with shredded Cheddar cheese and purchased precooked bacon bits. Sprinkle with smoked whole almonds; serve with your favorite dressing.

6 **Easy Fried Cheese and Mixed-Greens Salad:** Heat frozen breaded mozzarella cheese sticks as directed on package; cut each stick into fourths. Top salad greens with cheese stick pieces and halved cherry tomatoes; serve with your favorite dressing.

7 **Mango-Avocado-Raspberry Salad:** On a serving platter or individual serving plates, arrange ripe avocado and jarred mango slices; drizzle with purchased raspberry vinaigrette. Serve with freshly ground pepper.

8 **Pineapple and Honey-Nut Coleslaw:** Stir canned pineapple tidbits (drained) and honey-roasted peanuts into purchased creamy coleslaw.

9 **Melon and Berries with Vanilla Sauce:** On a serving platter, arrange sliced cantaloupe and honeydew melon; top with raspberries or blackberries. Mix together vanilla yogurt and milk until it has a saucy consistency; drizzle over fruit.

10 **Sunny Lime Fruit Salad:** Drizzle a variety of cut-up fruits with thawed frozen limeade concentrate. Toss in poppy seed or slivered almonds if desired.

This icon means: 🕐 **20 minutes or less**

Chicken and Ravioli Carbonara

2 tablespoons Italian dressing

1 lb boneless skinless chicken breasts,
cut into 1/2-inch strips

3/4 cup chicken broth

1 package (9 oz) refrigerated cheese-filled
ravioli

1/2 cup half-and-half

4 slices bacon, crisply cooked, crumbled

Shredded Parmesan cheese, if desired

Chopped fresh parsley, if desired

1 In 10-inch skillet, heat dressing over high heat. Cook chicken in dressing
2 to 4 minutes, turning occasionally, until brown.

2 Add broth and ravioli to skillet. Heat to boiling; reduce heat to medium.
Cook uncovered about 4 minutes or until ravioli are tender and almost all
broth has evaporated.

3 Stir in half-and-half; reduce heat. Simmer uncovered 3 to 5 minutes or
until sauce is hot and desired consistency (cook longer for a thicker sauce).
Sprinkle with bacon, cheese and parsley.

4 servings

Instant
Success!

*Betty Crocker Kitchens testing
often shows interesting results.
The less time this sauce is
cooked, the thinner it will be;
if cooked longer, the sauce
will become thick and coat the
ravioli. The choice is yours—
some people like to have more
sauce to dip their bread into!*

1 **Serving:** Calories 460 (Calories from Fat 190); Total Fat 21g (Saturated Fat 9g; Trans Fat 0g); Cholesterol 125mg;
Sodium 750mg; Total Carbohydrate 30g (Dietary Fiber 1g; Sugars 5g); Protein 38g ∾ **% Daily Value:** Vitamin A 6%;
Vitamin C 0%; Calcium 15%; Iron 15% ∾ **Exchanges:** 1 Starch, 1 Other Carbohydrate, 5 Very Lean Meat, 3 1/2 Fat
∾ **Carbohydrate Choices:** 2

Chicken and Garlic Ravioli with Peppers and Sun-Dried Tomatoes

2 packages (9 oz each) refrigerated chicken and roasted garlic-filled ravioli

1/2 cup julienne sun-dried tomatoes in oil and herbs (from 8-oz jar), drained, 2 tablespoons oil reserved

1 bag (1 lb) frozen bell pepper and onion stir-fry, thawed, drained

2 cups shredded provolone cheese (8 oz)

1 Cook and drain ravioli as directed on package.

2 In 12-inch skillet, heat reserved oil from tomatoes over medium heat. Cook bell pepper mixture in oil 2 minutes, stirring occasionally. Stir in tomatoes and ravioli. Cook, stirring occasionally, until hot.

3 Sprinkle with cheese; remove from heat. Cover; let stand 1 to 2 minutes or until cheese is melted.

6 servings

Instant **Success!**

Our best friends are always there for us, as it is with shredded mozzarella cheese— it's a great "pinch hitter" if you don't have provolone.

1 Serving: Calories 390 (Calories from Fat 170); Total Fat 19g (Saturated Fat 8g; Trans Fat 0g); Cholesterol 35mg; Sodium 540mg; Total Carbohydrate 35g (Dietary Fiber 3g; Sugars 7g); Protein 19g ✎ **% Daily Value:** Vitamin A 10%; Vitamin C 35%; Calcium 30%; Iron 10% ✎ **Exchanges:** 1 1/2 Starch, 1/2 Other Carbohydrate, 1 Vegetable, 2 High-Fat Meat, 1/2 Fat ✎ **Carbohydrate Choices:** 2

Prep Time **20 Minutes**
Start to Finish **20 Minutes**

Crispy Chicken and Fettuccine

1 package (12 oz) frozen southern-style chicken nuggets

1 package (9 oz) refrigerated fettuccine

1 can (14.5 oz) Italian-seasoned diced tomatoes, undrained

1 can (15 oz) tomato sauce

2 tablespoons chopped fresh parsley

2 tablespoons shredded Parmesan cheese

1 Heat oven to 400°F. Bake chicken nuggets as directed on package. If desired, cut chicken nuggets in half.

2 Meanwhile, cook and drain fettuccine as directed on package. Leave fettuccine in colander after draining. In same saucepan, heat tomatoes and tomato sauce over medium heat, stirring occasionally, until thoroughly heated.

3 Add fettuccine, chicken and parsley to tomato sauce; toss to coat. Sprinkle with cheese.

4 servings

Instant
Success!

"Gotta" love that refrigerated pasta! It cooks much more quickly than dried, so follow the directions on the package carefully.

1 Serving: Calories 530 (Calories from Fat 180); Total Fat 20g (Saturated Fat 5g; Trans Fat 2.5g); Cholesterol 55mg; Sodium 1490mg; Total Carbohydrate 58g (Dietary Fiber 5g; Sugars 8g); Protein 28g ✦ **% Daily Value:** Vitamin A 15%; Vitamin C 15%; Calcium 10%; Iron 30% ✦ **Exchanges:** 2 1/2 Starch, 1/2 Other Carbohydrate, 2 Vegetable, 2 1/2 High-Fat Meat ✦ **Carbohydrate Choices:** 4

Betty Crocker quick & easy cookbook

Pesto Turkey and Pasta

3 cups uncooked bow-tie (farfalle) pasta
(6 oz)

2 cups cubed cooked turkey breast

1/2 cup basil pesto

1/2 cup coarsely chopped roasted red bell
peppers (from 7-oz jar)

1/4 cup sliced ripe olives

1 In 3-quart saucepan, cook and drain pasta as directed on package.

2 In same saucepan, mix drained pasta, turkey, pesto and bell peppers. Heat
over low heat, stirring constantly, until hot. Garnish with olives.

4 servings

Speed it Up

*Can't boil water any faster,
right? Actually you can! Fill the
saucepan with hot tap water;
cover it and turn the burner on
high. Dinner's that much closer!*

1 Serving: Calories 430 (Calories from Fat 170); Total Fat 19g (Saturated Fat 3.5g; Trans Fat 0g); Cholesterol 65mg;
Sodium 530mg; Total Carbohydrate 37g (Dietary Fiber 4g; Sugars 2g); Protein 29g ✴ **% Daily Value:** Vitamin A 30%;
Vitamin C 35%; Calcium 15%; Iron 20% ✴ **Exchanges:** 2 1/2 Starch, 3 Lean Meat, 1 1/2 Fat ✴ **Carbohydrate
Choices:** 2 1/2

Betty Crocker quick & easy cookbook

Bow-Tie Pasta with Beef and Tomatoes

2 cups uncooked bow-tie (farfalle) pasta (4 oz)

1 tablespoon olive or vegetable oil

1 cup frozen bell pepper and onion stir-fry (from 1-lb bag)

1 lb beef strips for stir-fry or thinly sliced flank steak

1 can (14.5 oz) Italian-style stewed tomatoes, undrained

1 teaspoon garlic salt

1/4 teaspoon pepper

Fresh basil leaves, if desired

Freshly shredded Parmesan cheese, if desired

1 Cook and drain pasta as directed on package.

2 Meanwhile, in 12-inch skillet, heat oil over medium-high heat. Cook bell pepper mixture in oil 3 minutes, stirring frequently. Stir in beef. Cook 5 to 6 minutes, stirring frequently, until beef is no longer pink.

3 Stir in tomatoes, garlic salt and pepper. Cook 2 to 3 minutes, stirring frequently and breaking up tomatoes slightly with spoon, until mixture is hot. Stir in pasta. Cook 1 to 2 minutes, stirring constantly, until pasta is well coated and hot. Garnish with basil. Serve with cheese.

4 servings

Speed it Up

This handy one-dish pasta recipe is already fast, but it's even faster (and handier) if you substitute leftover cold pasta you might have in the fridge for the uncooked pasta. No need to warm it up first; just heat it an extra minute or two after stirring into the sauce.

1 Serving: Calories 350 (Calories from Fat 110); Total Fat 12g (Saturated Fat 3.5g; Trans Fat 0g); Cholesterol 50mg; Sodium 520mg; Total Carbohydrate 29g (Dietary Fiber 3g; Sugars 4g); Protein 31g ✌ **% Daily Value:** Vitamin A 4%; Vitamin C 20%; Calcium 6%; Iron 25% ✌ **Exchanges:** 1 1/2 Starch, 1 Vegetable, 3 1/2 Very Lean Meat, 2 Fat ✌ Carbohydrate Choices: 2

Orange Teriyaki Beef with Noodles

1 lb boneless beef sirloin, cut into thin strips

1 can (14 oz) beef broth

1/4 cup teriyaki stir-fry sauce

2 tablespoons orange marmalade

Dash ground red pepper (cayenne)

1 1/2 cups fresh snap pea pods

1 1/2 cups uncooked fine egg noodles (3 oz)

1 Spray 12-inch skillet with cooking spray; heat over medium-high heat. Cook beef in skillet 2 to 4 minutes, stirring occasionally, until brown. Remove beef from skillet; keep warm.

2 Add broth, stir-fry sauce, marmalade and red pepper to skillet. Heat to boiling. Stir in pea pods and noodles; reduce heat to medium. Cover and cook about 5 minutes or until noodles are tender.

3 Stir in beef. Cook uncovered 2 to 3 minutes or until sauce is slightly thickened.

4 servings

Instant Success!

Okay, you're not wild about orange marmalade, so use peach or apricot jam or preserves instead. For a side salad, pick up a bag of washed spinach and toss with mandarin orange segments. Drizzle with a favorite dressing and sprinkle with chopped green onions.

1 Serving: Calories 270 (Calories from Fat 40); Total Fat 4.5g (Saturated Fat 1.5g; Trans Fat 0g); Cholesterol 85mg; Sodium 1160mg; Total Carbohydrate 25g (Dietary Fiber 1g; Sugars 8g); Protein 31g ✒ **% Daily Value:** Vitamin A 6%; Vitamin C 10%; Calcium 4%; Iron 25% ✒ **Exchanges:** 1 Starch, 1/2 Other Carbohydrate, 4 Very Lean Meat, 1/2 Fat ✒ **Carbohydrate Choices:** 1 1/2

Parmesan Orzo and Meatballs

1 1/2 cups frozen bell pepper and onion stir-fry (from 1-lb bag)

2 tablespoons Italian dressing

1 can (14 oz) beef broth

1 cup uncooked orzo or rosamarina pasta (6 oz)

16 frozen cooked meatballs (from 16-oz bag)

1 large tomato, chopped (1 cup)

2 tablespoons chopped fresh parsley

1/4 cup shredded Parmesan cheese (1 oz)

1 In 12-inch nonstick skillet, cook bell pepper mixture and dressing over medium-high heat 2 minutes, stirring frequently.

2 Stir in broth; heat to boiling. Stir in pasta and meatballs. Heat to boiling; reduce heat to low. Cover; cook 10 minutes, stirring occasionally.

3 Stir in tomato. Cover; cook 3 to 5 minutes or until most of liquid has been absorbed and pasta is tender. Stir in parsley. Sprinkle with cheese.

4 servings

Instant **Success!**

Orzo is a rice-shaped pasta that cooks fairly quickly. It's also kid-friendly because it is easier to eat than long spaghetti.

1 Serving: Calories 360 (Calories from Fat 120); Total Fat 14g (Saturated Fat 4.5g; Trans Fat 0.5g); Cholesterol 65mg; Sodium 700mg; Total Carbohydrate 39g (Dietary Fiber 4g; Sugars 6g); Protein 21g ✻ **% Daily Value:** Vitamin A 15%; Vitamin C 25%; Calcium 15%; Iron 20% ✻ **Exchanges:** 1 1/2 Starch, 1/2 Other Carbohydrate, 1 Vegetable, 2 Medium-Fat Meat, 1/2 Fat ✻ **Carbohydrate Choices:** 2 1/2

Fettuccine with Italian Sausage and Olive Sauce

1 lb bulk Italian pork sausage

2 cans (14.5 oz each) diced tomatoes with basil, garlic and oregano, undrained

1 can (8 oz) tomato sauce

1/2 cup assorted small pitted olives

1 package (9 oz) refrigerated fettuccine

1/2 cup shredded Parmesan cheese (2 oz)

1 Heat water for cooking fettuccine to boiling. Meanwhile, in 12-inch skillet, cook sausage over medium-high heat 5 to 7 minutes, stirring occasionally, until no longer pink; drain if necessary.

2 Stir tomatoes, tomato sauce and olives into sausage. Reduce heat to low. Cover; cook 10 to 15 minutes, stirring occasionally, to blend flavors.

3 Cook and drain fettuccine as directed on package. Serve sauce over fettuccine. Sprinkle with cheese.

4 servings

Instant
Success!

Hot Italian sausage is a definite option here and would go especially well with the flavor of the olives, but if you live on the "mild" side, by all means, use the mild sweet version!

1 Serving: Calories 610 (Calories from Fat 260); Total Fat 29g (Saturated Fat 10g; Trans Fat 0g); Cholesterol 75mg; Sodium 2340mg; Total Carbohydrate 57g (Dietary Fiber 3g; Sugars 16g); Protein 32g ✎ **% Daily Value:** Vitamin A 15%; Vitamin C 25%; Calcium 30%; Iron 30% ✎ **Exchanges:** 2 1/2 Starch, 1 Other Carbohydrate, 1 Vegetable, 3 High-Fat Meat, 1/2 Fat ✎ **Carbohydrate Choices:** 4

Stove-Top Lasagna

Prep Time **20 Minutes**
Start to Finish **20 Minutes**

1 lb bulk Italian sausage

1 medium green bell pepper, sliced

1 package (8 oz) sliced mushrooms (3 cups)

1 medium onion, chopped (1/2 cup)

3 cups uncooked mini lasagna (mafalda) noodles (6 oz)

2 1/2 cups water

1/2 teaspoon Italian seasoning

1 jar (26 oz) chunky tomato pasta sauce (any variety)

1 cup shredded Italian cheese blend or mozzarella cheese (4 oz)

1 In 12-inch skillet or 4-quart Dutch oven, cook sausage, bell pepper, mushrooms and onion over medium-high heat, stirring occasionally, until sausage is no longer pink; drain.

2 Stir in remaining ingredients except cheese. Heat to boiling, stirring occasionally; reduce heat. Simmer uncovered about 10 minutes or until pasta is tender. Sprinkle with cheese.

6 servings

Speed it Up

Crumble, cook and drain sausage ahead to save time. Cooked and drained ground beef is a quick substitution for the sausage in this easy lasagna.

1 **Serving:** Calories 500 (Calories from Fat 210); Total Fat 24g (Saturated Fat 9g; Trans Fat 0g); Cholesterol 60mg; Sodium 1260mg; Total Carbohydrate 50g (Dietary Fiber 5g; Sugars 14g); Protein 22g ✌ **% Daily Value:** Vitamin A 15%; Vitamin C 25%; Calcium 15%; Iron 20% ✌ **Exchanges:** 2 1/2 Starch, 1 Other Carbohydrate, 2 High-Fat Meat, 1 Fat ✌ **Carbohydrate Choices:** 3

Prep Time **25 Minutes**

Start to Finish **25 Minutes**

Creamy Mushroom Tortelloni

2 packages (9 oz each) refrigerated
    portabello mushroom–filled tortelloni

2 tablespoons butter or margarine

1/4 cup Italian-style dry bread crumbs

1 container (8 oz) chive-and-onion cream
    cheese spread

1 cup half-and-half

2 tablespoons chopped fresh parsley

2 tablespoons chopped fresh basil leaves

1/2 teaspoon salt

1 In 4-quart saucepan or Dutch oven, cook and drain tortelloni as directed on package.

2 Meanwhile, in 8-inch skillet, melt butter over medium heat. Cook bread crumbs in butter 3 to 5 minutes, stirring occasionally, until golden brown; remove from heat.

3 Return drained tortelloni to saucepan. Reduce heat to medium-low. Gently stir in cream cheese spread, half-and-half, parsley, basil and salt until cheese is melted and mixture is hot, about 3 to 5 minutes. Spoon into individual serving dishes. Sprinkle buttered bread crumbs over tortelloni. Serve immediately.

5 servings

Instant **Success!**

Don't keep dry bread crumbs in your pantry? Two slices of bread can be crumbled by hand, or for a finer texture, whirled in a food processor.

1 **Serving:** Calories 560 (Calories from Fat 270); Total Fat 30g (Saturated Fat 18g; Trans Fat 1g); Cholesterol 105mg; Sodium 1120mg; Total Carbohydrate 54g (Dietary Fiber 3g; Sugars 10g); Protein 19g ✶ **% Daily Value:** Vitamin A 25%; Vitamin C 2%; Calcium 30%; Iron 20% ✶ **Exchanges:** 2 1/2 Starch, 1 Other Carbohydrate, 1 1/2 High-Fat Meat, 3 1/2 Fat ✶ **Carbohydrate Choices:** 3 1/2

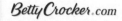
BettyCrocker.com

Pan-Fried Ravioli in Vodka Sauce

Prep Time **30 Minutes**
Start to Finish **30 Minutes**

1 bag (25 oz) frozen beef-filled ravioli

3 tablespoons extra-virgin olive oil

1 tablespoon butter or margarine

2 cloves garlic, finely chopped

3 plum (Roma) tomatoes, seeded, chopped

1 jar (25 to 26 oz) vodka pasta sauce

3/4 cup shredded Parmesan or Asiago cheese (3 oz)

1 In 6-quart Dutch oven, heat 4 quarts water to boiling. Add ravioli. Cook 3 minutes; drain.

2 In 12-inch nonstick skillet, heat 1 tablespoon of the oil and half of the butter over medium heat. Add half of the drained ravioli. Cook 3 to 4 minutes, stirring once or twice, until golden brown. Remove to large serving platter; cover to keep warm. Repeat with 1 tablespoon oil, the remaining butter and ravioli. Remove to platter.

3 To same skillet, add remaining 1 tablespoon oil and the garlic. Cook over medium heat 30 to 60 seconds, stirring occasionally, until garlic is tender. Stir in tomatoes. Cook 1 to 2 minutes, stirring constantly, until hot. Stir in pasta sauce. Cook 2 to 3 minutes, stirring once, until thoroughly heated.

4 Pour sauce over ravioli. Sprinkle with cheese.

6 servings

Instant Success!

If you can't find that yummy vodka pasta sauce at your grocery store, make your own by combining 1 jar (26 oz) tomato pasta sauce, 1/2 cup whipping cream and 2 tablespoons vodka.

1 Serving: Calories 500 (Calories from Fat 220); Total Fat 24g (Saturated Fat 8g; Trans Fat 0g); Cholesterol 155mg; Sodium 1730mg; Total Carbohydrate 50g (Dietary Fiber 4g; Sugars 13g); Protein 20g ⁓ **% Daily Value:** Vitamin A 60%; Vitamin C 15%; Calcium 30%; Iron 20% ⁓ **Exchanges:** 2 Starch, 1 Other Carbohydrate, 2 High-Fat Meat, 1 1/2 Fat ⁓ **Carbohydrate Choices:** 3

Shrimp Alfredo Primavera

3 cups uncooked bow-tie (farfalle) pasta
(6 oz)

2 slices bacon, cut into 1/2-inch pieces

1 1/2 cups frozen sweet peas
(from 1-lb bag)

1/4 cup water

1 lb uncooked deveined peeled medium
shrimp, thawed if frozen, tail shells
removed

3/4 cup refrigerated Alfredo sauce
(from 10-oz container)

2 tablespoons chopped fresh chives

1 Cook and drain pasta as directed on package.

2 Meanwhile, in 12-inch nonstick skillet, cook bacon over medium heat
4 to 5 minutes, stirring occasionally, until crisp. Stir in peas; cook 2 minutes,
stirring occasionally. Add water; cover and cook 3 to 5 minutes or until peas
are tender and water has evaporated. Add shrimp; cook 2 to 3 minutes, stirring
occasionally, until shrimp are pink.

3 Stir in Alfredo sauce and pasta. Cook over medium-low heat, stirring
occasionally, until thoroughly heated. Sprinkle with chives.

4 servings

Instant
Success!

*Using refrigerated Alfredo sauce
is only one option—the jarred
version can be used instead,
or lighten up if you wish by
using the reduced-fat version
of this creamy, cheesy sauce.*

1 Serving: Calories 450 (Calories from Fat 160); Total Fat 18g (Saturated Fat 10g; Trans Fat 0.5g); Cholesterol 210mg;
Sodium 650mg; Total Carbohydrate 43g (Dietary Fiber 4g; Sugars 3g); Protein 30g ∾ **% Daily Value:** Vitamin A 35%;
Vitamin C 6%; Calcium 15%; Iron 30% ∾ **Exchanges:** 2 Starch, 1 Other Carbohydrate, 3 Very Lean Meat, 3 Fat ∾
Carbohydrate Choices: 3

Tagliatelle Pasta with Asparagus and Gorgonzola Sauce

1 lb asparagus

8 oz uncooked tagliatelle pasta
    or fettuccine

2 tablespoons olive or vegetable oil

4 medium green onions, sliced (1/4 cup)

1/4 cup chopped fresh parsley

1 clove garlic, finely chopped

1 cup crumbled Gorgonzola cheese
    (4 oz)

1/2 teaspoon freshly cracked pepper

1 Break off tough ends of asparagus as far down as stalks snap easily. Cut asparagus into 1-inch pieces. Cook pasta as directed on package, adding asparagus during last 5 minutes of cooking; drain.

2 Meanwhile, in 12-inch skillet, heat oil over medium-high heat. Cook onions, parsley and garlic in oil about 5 minutes, stirring occasionally, until onions are tender. Reduce heat to medium.

3 Add pasta, asparagus and cheese to mixture in skillet. Cook about 3 minutes, tossing gently, until cheese is melted and pasta is evenly coated. Sprinkle with pepper.

4 servings

Speed it Up

Let your ingredients join forces! Adding vegetables to pasta water during the last minutes of cooking saves a major step (and saves you extra pans).

1 Serving: Calories 370 (Calories from Fat 160); Total Fat 17g (Saturated Fat 7g; Trans Fat 0g); Cholesterol 70mg; Sodium 640mg; Total Carbohydrate 40g (Dietary Fiber 3g; Sugars 2g); Protein 15g ✑ **% Daily Value:** Vitamin A 20%; Vitamin C 15%; Calcium 20%; Iron 20% ✑ **Exchanges:** 2 Starch, 1/2 Other Carbohydrate, 1 Vegetable, 1 High-Fat Meat, 1 1/2 Fat ✑ **Carbohydrate Choices:** 2 1/2

Penne with Spicy Sauce

Prep Time **30 Minutes**
Start to Finish **30 Minutes**

1 package (16 oz) penne pasta

1 can (28 oz) Italian-style peeled whole tomatoes, undrained

2 tablespoons olive or vegetable oil

2 cloves garlic, finely chopped

1 teaspoon crushed red pepper flakes

2 tablespoons chopped fresh parsley

1 tablespoon tomato paste (from 6-oz can)

1/2 cup freshly grated or shredded Parmesan cheese

1 Cook and drain pasta as directed on package. Meanwhile, in food processor or blender, place tomatoes with juice. Cover; process until coarsely chopped.

2 In 12-inch skillet, heat oil over medium-high heat. Cook garlic, red pepper flakes and parsley in oil about 5 minutes, stirring frequently, until garlic just begins to turn golden. Stir in chopped tomatoes and tomato paste. Heat to boiling; reduce heat. Cover; simmer about 10 minutes, stirring occasionally, until slightly thickened.

3 Add pasta and 1/4 cup of the cheese to mixture in skillet. Cook about 3 minutes, tossing gently, until pasta is evenly coated. Sprinkle with remaining 1/4 cup cheese.

6 servings

Instant
Success!

Not in the mood for a meatless red sauce? Add sliced pepperoni with the chopped tomatoes in step 2 for a new taste sensation.

1 Serving: Calories 400 (Calories from Fat 80); Total Fat 9g (Saturated Fat 2.5g; Trans Fat 0g); Cholesterol 5mg; Sodium 640mg; Total Carbohydrate 66g (Dietary Fiber 6g; Sugars 5g); Protein 15g ✂ **% Daily Value:** Vitamin A 8%; Vitamin C 10%; Calcium 15%; Iron 25% ✂ **Exchanges:** 4 Starch, 1 Vegetable, 1 1/2 Fat ✂ **Carbohydrate Choices:** 4 1/2

Prep Time **20 Minutes**
Start to Finish **20 Minutes**

Southwest Cheese 'n Pasta

2 2/3 cups uncooked cavatappi pasta
    (about 8 oz)

1 cup green salsa (salsa verde)

1 1/2 cups milk

1 can (14.75 oz) cream-style corn,
    undrained

1 can (11 oz) whole kernel corn with
    red and green peppers, drained

1 loaf (8 oz) prepared cheese product,
    cut into cubes

1 In 12-inch nonstick skillet, mix all ingredients except cheese. Heat to boiling, stirring occasionally; reduce heat to low. Cover; cook 10 to 14 minutes, stirring frequently, until pasta is tender.

2 Stir in cheese until melted.

6 servings

Easy Add-On

Ham it up for a heartier rendition of this cheesy dish! Add 2 cups of cubed cooked ham in step 1, and continue as directed.

1 Serving: Calories 420 (Calories from Fat 100); Total Fat 12g (Saturated Fat 6g; Trans Fat 0g); Cholesterol 35mg; Sodium 950mg; Total Carbohydrate 61g (Dietary Fiber 5g; Sugars 14g); Protein 17g ✂ **% Daily Value:** Vitamin A 15%; Vitamin C 30%; Calcium 25%; Iron 15% ✂ **Exchanges:** 3 Starch, 1 Other Carbohydrate, 1 High-Fat Meat, 1/2 Fat ✂ **Carbohydrate Choices:** 4

Betty Crocker quick & easy cookbook

Barbecue Chicken Pizza

Prep Time **10 Minutes**
Start to Finish **20 Minutes**

2 cups shredded rotisserie or other cooked chicken breast

1/3 cup barbecue sauce

1 package (10 oz) prebaked thin Italian pizza crust (12 inch)

3 plum (Roma) tomatoes, sliced

1 cup shredded Monterey Jack cheese (4 oz)

2 tablespoons chopped fresh cilantro leaves

1 Heat oven to 450°F. In small bowl, mix chicken and barbecue sauce. Place pizza crust on ungreased cookie sheet; spread chicken mixture over crust. Arrange tomatoes over chicken; sprinkle with cheese.

2 Bake 8 to 10 minutes or until cheese is melted and crust is browned. Sprinkle with cilantro.

6 servings

Speed it Up

On the move? Make barbecued chicken wraps! No baking needed! Instead of pizza crust, substitute 6 flour tortillas (6 to 8 inch). Spread chicken mixture evenly over wraps to within 1 inch of edge. Top with tomatoes, cheese and cilantro. Roll up tortillas tightly.

1 Serving: Calories 300 (Calories from Fat 100); Total Fat 11g (Saturated Fat 6g; Trans Fat 0g); Cholesterol 60mg; Sodium 710mg; Total Carbohydrate 27g (Dietary Fiber 1g; Sugars 5g); Protein 24g ✌ **% Daily Value:** Vitamin A 10%; Vitamin C 4%; Calcium 15%; Iron 10% ✌ **Exchanges:** 1 1/2 Starch, 1/2 Other Carbohydrate, 3 Lean Meat ✌ **Carbohydrate Choices:** 2

Prep Time **5 Minutes**
Start to Finish **15 Minutes**

Double-Cheese, Spinach and Chicken Pizza

1 package (14 oz) prebaked original Italian pizza crust (12 inch)

1 cup shredded Havarti cheese (4 oz)

2 cups washed fresh baby spinach leaves (from 10-oz bag)

1 cup diced rotisserie or other cooked chicken

1/4 cup chopped drained roasted red bell peppers (from 7-oz jar)

1/2 teaspoon garlic salt

1 cup shredded Cheddar cheese (4 oz)

1 Heat oven to 425°F. Place pizza crust on ungreased cookie sheet.

2 Top with Havarti cheese, spinach, chicken, bell peppers, garlic salt and Cheddar cheese.

3 Bake 8 to 10 minutes or until crust is golden brown.

6 servings

Speed it Up

Why not buy bags of fresh spinach and shredded cheese? All the hard work is already done. By the way, you can use most any type of cheese in place of Havarti.

1 Serving: Calories 380 (Calories from Fat 170); Total Fat 19g (Saturated Fat 11g; Trans Fat 0.5g); Cholesterol 70mg; Sodium 800mg; Total Carbohydrate 30g (Dietary Fiber 2g; Sugars 1g); Protein 23g ❧ **% Daily Value:** Vitamin A 40%; Vitamin C 15%; Calcium 25%; Iron 15% ❧ **Exchanges:** 2 Starch, 2 1/2 Lean Meat, 2 Fat ❧ **Carbohydrate Choices:** 2

Betty Crocker quick & easy cookbook

Easy Philly Cheesesteak Pizza

1 can (13.8 oz) refrigerated pizza crust

2 cups frozen bell pepper and onion stir-fry (from 1-lb bag)

2 tablespoons creamy Dijon mustard-mayonnaise spread

8 oz thinly sliced cooked roast beef (from deli)

2 cups shredded American cheese (8 oz)

1 Heat oven to 425°F. Spray 12-inch pizza pan with cooking spray. Press pizza crust dough in pan. Bake 8 minutes.

2 Meanwhile, spray 10-inch skillet with cooking spray; heat over medium-high heat. Cook bell pepper mixture in skillet 4 to 5 minutes, stirring frequently, until crisp-tender; drain if necessary.

3 Spread mustard-mayonnaise spread over partially baked crust. Top with roast beef, bell pepper mixture and cheese. Bake 8 to 10 minutes or until crust is golden brown.

6 servings

Instant **Success!**

Here's a quick take on the cheesesteak sandwich made famous in Philadelphia in the 1930s. Turning it into a hearty pizza means it can serve the whole family super-fast.

1 **Serving:** Calories 420 (Calories from Fat 180); Total Fat 20g (Saturated Fat 10g; Trans Fat 0.5g); Cholesterol 65mg; Sodium 1130mg; Total Carbohydrate 37g (Dietary Fiber 0g; Sugars 6g); Protein 23g ✷ **% Daily Value:** Vitamin A 8%; Vitamin C 15%; Calcium 20%; Iron 15% ✷ **Exchanges:** 1 1/2 Starch, 1/2 Other Carbohydrate, 1 Vegetable, 2 1/2 High-Fat Meat ✷ **Carbohydrate Choices:** 2 1/2

Betty Crocker quick & easy cookbook

Shrimp and Feta Pizza

Prep Time **10 Minutes**
Start to Finish **25 Minutes**

1 package (14 oz) prebaked original
  Italian pizza crust (12 inch)

1 tablespoon olive or vegetable oil

1/2 lb uncooked deveined peeled medium
  shrimp, thawed if frozen, tail shells
  removed

1 clove garlic, finely chopped

2 cups shredded mozzarella cheese (8 oz)

1 can (2 1/4 oz) sliced ripe olives, drained

1 cup crumbled feta cheese (4 oz)

1 tablespoon chopped fresh or 1 teaspoon
  dried rosemary leaves

1 Heat oven to 400°F. Place pizza crust on ungreased cookie sheet.

2 In 10-inch nonstick skillet, heat oil over medium heat. Cook shrimp and
garlic in oil about 3 minutes, stirring frequently, until shrimp are pink.

3 Sprinkle 1 cup of the mozzarella cheese over pizza crust. Top with shrimp,
olives, remaining 1 cup mozzarella cheese and the feta cheese. Sprinkle with
rosemary. Bake 12 to 15 minutes or until cheese is melted.

6 servings

Instant
Success!

*Who says you need tomato
sauces on pizza? This classy
version features two kinds
of cheese and succulent
shrimp, and it's a mouthful!*

1 Serving: Calories 400 (Calories from Fat 170); Total Fat 19g (Saturated Fat 10g; Trans Fat 0.5g); Cholesterol 100mg;
Sodium 890mg; Total Carbohydrate 32g (Dietary Fiber 2g; Sugars 1g); Protein 25g ✻ % **Daily Value:** Vitamin A 10%;
Vitamin C 0%; Calcium 40%; Iron 20% ✻ **Exchanges:** 2 Starch, 3 Very Lean Meat, 3 Fat ✻ **Carbohydrate Choices:** 2

Antipasto French Bread Pizzas

1 loaf (12 inch) French bread, cut in half horizontally

1/4 cup basil pesto

10 slices salami (3 1/2 inches in diameter)

2 or 3 plum (Roma) tomatoes, thinly sliced

1 small green bell pepper, cut into thin rings

2 medium green onions, chopped (2 tablespoons)

1/4 cup sliced ripe olives

6 slices (1 1/2 oz each) provolone cheese

1 Heat oven to 425°F. Place bread halves, cut sides up, on ungreased cookie sheet. Spread with pesto. Top with salami, tomatoes, bell pepper, onions, olives and cheese.

2 Bake 8 to 10 minutes or until cheese is melted.

6 servings

Instant
Success!

You know what they say: variety is the spice of life! For some quick substitutions, use pepperoni slices instead of salami and sliced or shredded mozzarella cheese for the provolone. No plum tomatoes today? Thinly slice regular tomatoes.

1 Serving: Calories 380 (Calories from Fat 220); Total Fat 24g (Saturated Fat 11g; Trans Fat 0.5g); Cholesterol 45mg; Sodium 1030mg; Total Carbohydrate 22g (Dietary Fiber 2g; Sugars 2g); Protein 19g ✎ **% Daily Value:** Vitamin A 15%; Vitamin C 10%; Calcium 40%; Iron 10% ✎ **Exchanges:** 1 1/2 Starch, 2 High-Fat Meat, 1 1/2 Fat ✎ **Carbohydrate Choices:** 1 1/2

Betty Crocker quick & easy cookbook

White Bean and Spinach Pizza

2 cups water

1/2 cup sun-dried tomato halves
(not oil-packed)

1 can (15 to 16 oz) great northern
or navy beans, drained, rinsed

2 medium cloves garlic, finely chopped

1 package (14 oz) prebaked original
Italian pizza crust (12 inch)

1/4 teaspoon dried oregano leaves

1 cup firmly packed spinach leaves,
shredded

1/2 cup shredded Colby–Monterey Jack
cheese blend (2 oz)

1 Heat oven to 425°F. Heat water to boiling. In small bowl, pour enough boiling water over dried tomatoes to cover. Let stand 10 minutes; drain. Cut into thin strips; set aside.

2 In food processor, place beans and garlic. Cover; process until smooth.

3 Place pizza crust on ungreased cookie sheet. Spread beans over pizza crust. Sprinkle with oregano, tomatoes, spinach and cheese. Bake 8 to 10 minutes or until cheese is melted.

8 servings

Instant Success!

In an extra bit of a hurry? Use a 7-ounce container of roasted garlic or regular hummus instead of processing the canned beans and garlic cloves in the food processor.

1 Serving: Calories 240 (Calories from Fat 50); Total Fat 6g (Saturated Fat 3g; Trans Fat 0g); Cholesterol 10mg; Sodium 370mg; Total Carbohydrate 36g (Dietary Fiber 4g; Sugars 2g); Protein 12g ✱ **% Daily Value:** Vitamin A 10%; Vitamin C 2%; Calcium 10%; Iron 20% ✱ **Exchanges:** 2 1/2 Starch, 1/2 Lean Meat, 1/2 Fat ✱ **Carbohydrate Choices:** 2 1/2

6 soup & hot sandwiches

Quick Ideas for Bread

Any way you slice it, bread can make the meal—kick it way up by topping it with one of these great options.

1 **Ranch–Parmesan Cheese Toasts:** Spread cut sides of hot dog buns with ranch dressing; sprinkle with grated Parmesan cheese. Broil with tops 4 to 6 inches from heat 1 to 2 minutes or until topping begins to bubble.

2 **Cheddar and Garlic "Saucers":** Spread cut sides of hamburger buns with softened butter; sprinkle with garlic powder or garlic salt and shredded Cheddar cheese. Broil with tops 4 to 6 inches from heat 1 to 2 minutes or until cheese is melted.

3 **Smoked Cheddar and Almond Focaccia:** Heat oven to 375°F. On an ungreased cookie sheet, place 12-inch prebaked thin Italian pizza crust. Spread crust lightly with honey mustard; sprinkle with shredded smoked Cheddar or Gouda cheese and sliced almonds. Bake 15 to 20 minutes or until cheese is melted.

4 **Soft Italian Breadsticks:** Brush purchased soft breadsticks with olive oil; sprinkle with Italian seasoning and grated Parmesan cheese. Heat in oven as directed on breadstick package.

5 **Spinach Dip Crostini:** On an ungreased cookie sheet, place 1-inch slices of French bread. Broil with tops 4 to 6 inches from heat 30 to 60 seconds or until lightly toasted. Spread each slice with purchased spinach dip; sprinkle with shredded mozzarella or Asiago cheese. Broil 1 to 2 minutes longer or until cheese is melted.

6 **Pesto-Parmesan Loaf:** Cut a 1-pound loaf of French bread horizontally in half; place with cut sides up on an ungreased cookie sheet. Broil with tops 4 to 6 inches from heat about 1 minute or until lightly toasted. Spread toasted sides with basil pesto; sprinkle with shredded Parmesan cheese. Broil 1 to 2 minutes longer or until cheese is melted.

7 **Singing-the-Blues Garlic Bread:** Sprinkle bottom half of a purchased garlic bread loaf with crumbled blue cheese; replace the top. Heat as directed on package.

8 **Texas Toast:** Spread one side of Texas toast bread or thickly sliced bread (about 1 inch) with softened butter; sprinkle with barbecue seasoning. Broil with tops 4 to 6 inches from heat 30 to 60 seconds or until lightly toasted.

9 **Corn Muffins with Maple Butter:** Beat 1/2 cup softened butter with electric mixer until light and fluffy; beat in 1/2 cup maple syrup until well mixed and creamy. Serve with heated corn muffins or cornbread squares.

10 **Warm Tortillas with Lime Butter:** Mix melted butter with grated lime peel; brush over warm tortillas. Fold tortillas in half and then in half again, or roll them up.

This icon means: ⏱ **20 minutes or less**

After-Work Chicken Noodle Soup

2 cups cut-up rotisserie or other cooked chicken

2 medium stalks celery, chopped (1 cup)

2 medium carrots, sliced (1 cup)

1 medium onion, chopped (1/2 cup)

1 tablespoon chopped fresh parsley or 1 teaspoon parsley flakes

1 teaspoon dried thyme leaves

1/4 teaspoon pepper

2 cloves garlic, finely chopped

4 cans (14 oz each) chicken broth

1 cup uncooked wide egg noodles (2 oz)

1 In 3-quart saucepan, heat all ingredients except noodles to boiling. Stir in noodles. Heat to boiling; reduce heat.

2 Simmer uncovered 8 to 10 minutes, stirring occasionally, until noodles and vegetables are tender.

4 servings

Speed it Up

This recipe is pretty streamlined, but here are a couple of tricks to make it even quicker. Use about 2 tablespoons plus 1 teaspoon chicken bouillon granules and 4 cups of water instead of getting out the can opener for the canned chicken broth. And substitute 1/4 to 1/2 teaspoon garlic powder to skip chopping fresh garlic.

1 Serving: Calories 260 (Calories from Fat 70); Total Fat 8g (Saturated Fat 2g; Trans Fat 0g); Cholesterol 70mg; Sodium 2070mg; Total Carbohydrate 17g (Dietary Fiber 2g; Sugars 3g); Protein 30g ✎ **% Daily Value:** Vitamin A 80%; Vitamin C 4%; Calcium 6%; Iron 15% ✎ **Exchanges:** 1 Starch, 4 Very Lean Meat, 1 Fat ✎ **Carbohydrate Choices:** 1

Chicken Cordon Bleu Chowder

Prep Time **15 Minutes**
Start to Finish **15 Minutes**

2 cans (18.8 oz each) ready-to-serve creamy potato with roasted garlic soup

1 cup cut-up rotisserie or other cooked chicken

1 cup diced cooked ham

1 cup shredded Swiss cheese (4 oz)

1 tablespoon chopped fresh chives

1 In 3-quart saucepan, heat soup, chicken and ham over medium heat 5 minutes, stirring occasionally.

2 Slowly stir in cheese. Cook about 2 minutes, stirring frequently, until cheese is melted. Serve topped with chives.

4 servings

Instant **Success!**

Chicken or veal cordon bleu is a traditional dish that rolls chicken breasts or veal around Swiss cheese and ham. This lively trio has been morphed into a hearty chowder that's so good! Use all ham or all chicken if that's what you have on hand.

1 Serving: Calories 460 (Calories from Fat 260); Total Fat 29g (Saturated Fat 11g; Trans Fat 0g); Cholesterol 100mg; Sodium 1640mg; Total Carbohydrate 19g (Dietary Fiber 2g; Sugars 1g); Protein 32g ✖ **% Daily Value:** Vitamin A 8%; Vitamin C 6%; Calcium 25%; Iron 8% ✖ **Exchanges:** 1 1/2 Starch, 4 Lean Meat, 3 Fat ✖ **Carbohydrate Choices:** 1

soup & **hot sandwiches**

Beef 'n Veggie Soup with Mozzarella

1 lb lean (at least 80%) ground beef

1 large onion, chopped (1 cup)

2 cups frozen mixed vegetables
(from 1-lb bag)

1 can (14.5 oz) diced tomatoes with
green pepper, celery and onions
(or other variety), undrained

4 cups water

5 teaspoons beef bouillon granules

1 1/2 teaspoons Italian seasoning

1/4 teaspoon pepper

1 cup shredded mozzarella cheese
(4 oz)

1 In 4-quart Dutch oven, cook beef and onion over medium-high heat 5 to 7 minutes, stirring occasionally, until beef is brown; drain.

2 Stir in remaining ingredients except cheese. Heat to boiling; reduce heat. Simmer uncovered 6 to 8 minutes, stirring occasionally, until vegetables are tender.

3 Sprinkle about 2 tablespoons cheese in each of 8 soup bowls; fill bowls with soup.

8 servings

Make it a Meal

Add some hearty rustic sour-dough or Italian rolls for dipping into the soup and a Caesar salad kit for chilly, crunchy goodness and that, my friend, is supper!

1 Serving: Calories 200 (Calories from Fat 80); Total Fat 9g (Saturated Fat 4.5g; Trans Fat 0g); Cholesterol 45mg; Sodium 790mg; Total Carbohydrate 13g (Dietary Fiber 3g; Sugars 5g); Protein 16g ❧ **% Daily Value:** Vitamin A 40%; Vitamin C 6%; Calcium 15%; Iron 10% ❧ **Exchanges:** 1/2 Other Carbohydrate, 1 Vegetable, 2 Medium-Fat Meat ❧ **Carbohydrate Choices:** 1

Asian Pork and Noodle Soup

1 lb boneless pork sirloin or loin, cut into 1/2-inch pieces

2 cloves garlic, finely chopped

2 teaspoons finely chopped gingerroot

2 cans (14 oz each) chicken broth

2 cups water

2 tablespoons soy sauce

2 cups uncooked fine egg noodles (4 oz)

1 medium carrot, sliced (1/2 cup)

1 small red bell pepper, chopped (1/2 cup)

2 cups fresh spinach leaves

1 Spray 3-quart saucepan with cooking spray; heat over medium-high heat. Add pork, garlic and gingerroot; cook 3 to 5 minutes, stirring frequently, until pork is brown.

2 Stir in broth, water and soy sauce. Heat to boiling; reduce heat. Simmer uncovered 5 minutes. Stir in noodles, carrot and bell pepper. Simmer uncovered about 10 minutes or until noodles are tender.

3 Stir in spinach; cook until thoroughly heated.

5 servings

Speed it Up

There always seems to be a way to make things faster! For this recipe, instead of cutting up the pork yourself, buy pork chow mein meat, which is already cut up and ready to go.

1 Serving: Calories 260 (Calories from Fat 80); Total Fat 9g (Saturated Fat 3g; Trans Fat 0g); Cholesterol 75mg; Sodium 1100mg; Total Carbohydrate 19g (Dietary Fiber 2g; Sugars 2g); Protein 26g ❧ **% Daily Value:** Vitamin A 60%; Vitamin C 30%; Calcium 4%; Iron 15% ❧ **Exchanges:** 1 Starch, 1 Vegetable, 3 Lean Meat ❧ **Carbohydrate Choices:** 1

Betty Crocker quick & easy cookbook

Italian Tomato Soup with Pesto-Cheese Toasts

1 cup water

2 cans (14 oz each) diced tomatoes with Italian herbs, undrained

1 can (11.5 oz) tomato juice

4 slices rosemary, Italian or French bread, 1/2 inch thick

2 tablespoons basil pesto

2 tablespoons shredded Parmesan cheese

1 In 3-quart saucepan, heat water, tomatoes and tomato juice to boiling.

2 Set oven control to broil. Place bread on cookie sheet. Spread with pesto; sprinkle with cheese. Broil with tops 4 to 6 inches from heat 1 to 2 minutes or until edges of bread are golden brown.

3 Into 4 soup bowls, ladle soup. Top each serving with bread slice.

4 servings

Make it a Meal

Take creative license! Turn this into a pizza soup by stirring in 1 pound of browned (drained) Italian sausage and a 2.5-ounce can of sliced mushrooms (drained) in step 1. Add a simple tossed salad with dressing, and you're good to go.

1 Serving: Calories 260 (Calories from Fat 60); Total Fat 7g (Saturated Fat 2g; Trans Fat 0g); Cholesterol 0mg; Sodium 910mg; Total Carbohydrate 39g (Dietary Fiber 4g; Sugars 8g); Protein 9g ✒ **% Daily Value:** Vitamin A 15%; Vitamin C 30%; Calcium 20%; Iron 25% ✒ **Exchanges:** 1 1/2 Starch, 1/2 Other Carbohydrate, 2 Vegetable, 1 1/2 Fat ✒ **Carbohydrate Choices:** 2 1/2

Prep Time **20 Minutes**
Start to Finish **20 Minutes**

Southwest Cheese Soup

1 loaf (1 lb) prepared cheese product,
    cut into cubes

1 can (15.25 oz) whole kernel corn,
    drained

1 can (15 oz) black beans, drained, rinsed

1 can (10 oz) diced tomatoes with
    green chiles, undrained

1 cup milk

Fresh cilantro sprigs, if desired

1 In 4-quart saucepan, mix all ingredients except cilantro.

2 Cook over medium-low heat 10 to 15 minutes, stirring frequently, until cheese is melted and soup is hot. Garnish each serving with cilantro.

4 servings

Make it
a **Meal**

*Enjoy this unbelievably easy
cheese soup with warm cornbread.*

1 Serving: Calories 610 (Calories from Fat 250); Total Fat 28g (Saturated Fat 17g; Trans Fat 0.5g); Cholesterol 95mg; Sodium 2130mg; Total Carbohydrate 59g (Dietary Fiber 9g; Sugars 23g); Protein 32g ⁓ **% Daily Value:** Vitamin A 35%; Vitamin C 10%; Calcium 70%; Iron 20% ⁓ **Exchanges:** 2 1/2 Starch, 1 1/2 Other Carbohydrate, 3 1/2 Medium-Fat Meat, 1 1/2 Fat ⁓ **Carbohydrate Choices:** 4

Betty Crocker quick & easy cookbook

Cincinnati Chili

10 oz uncooked spaghetti

1 lb lean (at least 80%) ground beef

1 medium onion, chopped (1/2 cup)

1 clove garlic, finely chopped

1 jar (26 to 28 oz) chunky vegetable-style
tomato pasta sauce

1 can (15 to 16 oz) kidney beans, drained,
rinsed

2 tablespoons chili powder

1/2 cup shredded Cheddar cheese (2 oz),
if desired

3 medium green onions, sliced, if desired

1 Cook and drain spaghetti as directed on package. Meanwhile, in 10-inch skillet, cook beef, onion and garlic over medium heat 8 to 10 minutes, stirring occasionally, until beef is brown; drain.

2 Stir pasta sauce, beans and chili powder into beef; reduce heat. Simmer uncovered 10 minutes, stirring occasionally. Serve sauce over spaghetti. Sprinkle with cheese and green onions.

6 servings

Speed it Up

Thin spaghetti and vermicelli both cook more quickly than regular spaghetti, so if you like pasta but need to shave minutes, try one of these options.

1 Serving: Calories 550 (Calories from Fat 130); Total Fat 14g (Saturated Fat 4g; Trans Fat 0.5g); Cholesterol 45mg; Sodium 860mg; Total Carbohydrate 78g (Dietary Fiber 10g; Sugars 13g); Protein 27g ❧ **% Daily Value:** Vitamin A 25%; Vitamin C 15%; Calcium 8%; Iron 35% ❧ **Exchanges:** 4 Starch, 1 Other Carbohydrate, 1 Vegetable, 2 Medium-Fat Meat ❧ **Carbohydrate Choices:** 5

Betty Crocker quick & easy cookbook

Zesty Autumn Pork Stew

Prep Time **25 Minutes**
Start to Finish **25 Minutes**

Cooking spray

1 lb pork tenderloin, cut into 1-inch cubes

2 medium dark-orange sweet potatoes, peeled, cubed (2 cups)

1 medium green bell pepper, chopped (1 cup)

2 cloves garlic, finely chopped

1 cup coleslaw mix (shredded cabbage and carrots)

1 teaspoon Cajun seasoning

1 can (14 oz) chicken broth

1 Spray 4-quart Dutch oven with cooking spray; heat over medium-high heat. Cook pork in Dutch oven, stirring occasionally, until brown.

2 Stir in remaining ingredients. Heat to boiling; reduce heat. Cover; simmer about 15 minutes, stirring once, until sweet potatoes are tender.

4 servings

Instant
Success!

Canned vacuum-packed sweet potatoes, cubed, can be substituted for the fresh sweet potatoes. Add them after you reduce the heat in step 2, and remember to stir the mixture gently, because canned sweet potatoes are very soft and tender.

1 Serving: Calories 240 (Calories from Fat 45); Total Fat 5g (Saturated Fat 1.5g; Trans Fat 0g); Cholesterol 70mg; Sodium 640mg; Total Carbohydrate 18g (Dietary Fiber 3g; Sugars 7g); Protein 30g ⁓ **% Daily Value:** Vitamin A 280%; Vitamin C 40%; Calcium 4%; Iron 15% ⁓ **Exchanges:** 1 Starch, 4 Very Lean Meat, 1/2 Fat ⁓ **Carbohydrate Choices:** 1

Old-Time Beef and Vegetable Stew

1 lb boneless beef sirloin steak,
    cut into 1/2-inch cubes

1 bag (1 lb) frozen stew vegetables,
    thawed, drained

1 can (15 oz) thick-and-zesty seasoned
    or plain tomato sauce

1 can (14 oz) beef broth

2 cans (5.5 oz each) spicy hot
    vegetable juice

1 Spray 10-inch skillet with cooking spray; heat over medium-high heat.
Cook beef in skillet about 10 minutes, stirring occasionally, until brown.

2 Stir in remaining ingredients. Heat to boiling; reduce heat. Cover; simmer
5 minutes, stirring occasionally.

6 servings

Instant
Success!

*A bag of frozen stew
vegetables—potatoes, carrots,
onions and peas—is really
handy for this recipe. The
size of the veggie pieces
varies from brand to brand,
but all will be done by the
end of the cooking time.*

1 Serving: Calories 170 (Calories from Fat 25); Total Fat 3g (Saturated Fat 1g, Trans Fat 0g); Cholesterol 45mg;
Sodium 850mg; Total Carbohydrate 16g (Dietary Fiber 3g, Sugars 7g); Protein 20g ✌ **% Daily Value:** Vitamin A 110%;
Vitamin C 20%; Calcium 4%; Iron 20% ✌ **Exchanges:** 1 Starch, 2 1/2 Very Lean Meat ✌ **Carbohydrate Choices:** 1

Caesar Chicken Paninis

Prep Time **30 Minutes**
Start to Finish **30 Minutes**

4 boneless skinless chicken breasts
(about 1 1/4 lb)

4 hard rolls (about 5 × 3 inches), split

4 slices red onion

1 large tomato, sliced

1/3 cup Caesar dressing

1/4 cup shredded Parmesan cheese
(1 oz)

4 leaves romaine lettuce

1 Between pieces of plastic wrap or waxed paper, place each chicken breast smooth side down; gently pound with flat side of meat mallet or rolling pin until about 1/4 inch thick.

2 Spray 8- or 10-inch skillet with cooking spray; heat over medium-high heat. Cook chicken in skillet 10 to 15 minutes, turning once, until chicken is no longer pink in center. Remove chicken from skillet; keep warm.

3 In skillet, place rolls, cut sides down. Cook over medium heat about 2 minutes or until toasted. Place chicken on bottom halves of rolls. Top with onion, tomato, dressing, cheese, lettuce and tops of rolls.

4 sandwiches

Instant
Success!

For kid-friendly crispy chicken paninis, nix the boneless skinless chicken breasts and steps 1 and 2, and instead, heat frozen breaded chicken patties per package directions and continue with the recipe in step 3.

1 Sandwich: Calories 500 (Calories from Fat 180); Total Fat 20g (Saturated Fat 4.5g; Trans Fat 1g); Cholesterol 90mg; Sodium 750mg; Total Carbohydrate 37g (Dietary Fiber 3g; Sugars 3g); Protein 41g ✧ **% Daily Value:** Vitamin A 25%; Vitamin C 15%; Calcium 15%; Iron 20% ✧ **Exchanges:** 2 Starch, 1 Vegetable, 4 1/2 Very Lean Meat, 3 1/2 Fat ✧ Carbohydrate Choices: 2 1/2

Montana Paninis

12 slices turkey bacon

1 small avocado, pitted, peeled

1/4 cup ranch dressing

12 slices sourdough bread, 1/2 inch thick

3 tablespoons butter or margarine,
    softened

3/4 lb thinly sliced cooked turkey (from
    deli)

1 large tomato, sliced

6 slices (1 oz each) Colby–Monterey Jack
    cheese blend

1 In 10-inch skillet, cook bacon over medium heat 8 to 10 minutes, turning occasionally, until crisp and brown. Remove from skillet; drain on paper towels. Break bacon slices in half.

2 In small bowl, mash avocado. Stir in dressing.

3 Spread one side of each bread slice with butter. Place 6 bread slices with buttered sides down; top with turkey, bacon, tomato, cheese and avocado mixture. Top with remaining bread slices, buttered sides up.

4 In 12-inch skillet, place sandwiches. Cover; cook over medium heat 4 to 5 minutes, turning once, until bread is crisp and cheese is melted.

6 sandwiches

Instant
Success!

Slash a little fat by trying turkey bacon. It has the same smoky flavor as pork bacon but much less fat. One slice of regular bacon weighs in at about 6 grams of fat per slice, versus turkey bacon at roughly 1/2 gram of fat per slice.

1 Sandwich: Calories 630 (Calories from Fat 320); Total Fat 36g (Saturated Fat 14g; Trans Fat 1.5g); Cholesterol 100mg; Sodium 2020mg; Total Carbohydrate 43g (Dietary Fiber 4g; Sugars 4g); Protein 32g ❧ **% Daily Value:** Vitamin A 15%; Vitamin C 6%; Calcium 30%; Iron 20% ❧ **Exchanges:** 2 Starch, 1 Other Carbohydrate, 3 1/2 Lean Meat, 5 Fat ❧ **Carbohydrate Choices:** 3

Prep Time **20 Minutes**
Start to Finish **20 Minutes**

Chicken Fajita Wraps

1 tablespoon chili powder

1 teaspoon salt

1 1/4 lb boneless skinless chicken breasts, cut into thin strips

1 tablespoon vegetable oil

1 bag (1 lb) frozen broccoli, red peppers, onions and mushrooms (or other combination)

8 flour tortillas (8 inch)

Salsa, if desired

1 In large bowl, sprinkle chili powder and salt over chicken; toss.

2 In 12-inch skillet, heat oil over high heat. Cook chicken in oil 3 to 4 minutes, stirring frequently, until no longer pink in center. Stir in vegetables. Cook about 4 minutes, stirring frequently, until vegetables are crisp-tender.

3 Onto center of each tortilla, spoon about 1/2 cup of the chicken mixture. Fold top and bottom ends of each tortilla about 1 inch over filling; fold right and left sides over folded ends, overlapping. Serve with salsa.

4 sandwiches

Instant
Success!

It's all about options. If you can't find the frozen veggie combo suggested, try a 1-pound bag of frozen corn, broccoli and sweet red peppers or any of your favorites.

1 Sandwich: Calories 520 (Calories from Fat 130); Total Fat 15g (Saturated Fat 3.5g; Trans Fat 1g); Cholesterol 85mg; Sodium 1370mg; Total Carbohydrate 56g (Dietary Fiber 5g; Sugars 3g); Protein 42g ❧ **% Daily Value:** Vitamin A 30%; Vitamin C 35%; Calcium 15%; Iron 30% ❧ **Exchanges:** 3 1/2 Starch, 1 Vegetable, 4 Very Lean Meat, 2 Fat ❧ **Carbohydrate Choices:** 4

Betty Crocker quick & easy cookbook

Italian Steak Sandwiches

1 tablespoon butter or margarine

1 medium onion, thinly sliced

4 beef cube steaks (about 1 1/2 lb)

1/2 teaspoon salt

1/4 teaspoon pepper

1/4 cup basil pesto

4 kaiser buns, split (toasted in oven if desired)

4 slices (about 3/4 oz each) mozzarella cheese

1 medium tomato, thinly sliced

1 In 12-inch nonstick skillet, melt butter over medium-high heat. Cook onion in butter 3 to 4 minutes, stirring frequently, until tender; push to side of skillet.

2 Add beef steaks to skillet; sprinkle with salt and pepper. Cook 5 to 8 minutes, turning once, for medium doneness (160°F).

3 Spread pesto on cut sides of buns. Layer steaks, cheese, onion and tomato in buns.

4 sandwiches

Instant Success!

Have you ever thought of putting that killer spinach dip you can buy from the deli or refrigerated case on a sandwich? Try it if you don't have the pesto on hand. Pick up a tub of potato salad or some other wonderful concoction from the deli to go with these sandwiches.

1 Sandwich: Calories 600 (Calories from Fat 260); Total Fat 29g (Saturated Fat 11g; Trans Fat 1.5g); Cholesterol 95mg; Sodium 880mg; Total Carbohydrate 32g (Dietary Fiber 2g; Sugars 3g); Protein 52g ✷ % Daily Value: Vitamin A 10%; Vitamin C 6%; Calcium 25%; Iron 30% ✷ Exchanges: 2 Starch, 6 1/2 Very Lean Meat, 5 Fat ✷ Carbohydrate Choices: 2

Peppered Pork Pitas
with Garlic Spread

1/3 cup mayonnaise or salad dressing

2 tablespoons milk

2 cloves garlic, finely chopped

1 lb boneless pork loin chops, cut into thin
   bite-size strips

1 tablespoon olive or vegetable oil

1 teaspoon coarsely ground pepper

1 jar (7 oz) roasted red bell peppers,
   drained, sliced

4 pita fold breads (7 inch)

1 In small bowl, mix mayonnaise, milk and garlic; set aside.

2 In medium bowl, mix pork, oil and pepper. Heat 12-inch skillet over
medium-high heat. Cook pork in skillet 5 to 6 minutes, stirring occasionally,
until pork is lightly browned on outside and no longer pink in center. Stir in
bell peppers; heat until warm.

3 Heat pita folds as directed on package. Lightly spread one side of each pita
fold with garlic mixture. Spoon pork mixture over each; fold up.

4 sandwiches

Speed it Up

*Speed it up by using jarred
chopped garlic and pork chow
mein meat instead of fresh
garlic and the pork chops.*

1 **Sandwich:** Calories 550 (Calories from Fat 250); Total Fat 27g (Saturated Fat 6g; Trans Fat 0g); Cholesterol 75mg;
Sodium 520mg; Total Carbohydrate 44g (Dietary Fiber 2g; Sugars 5g); Protein 32g ❧ **% Daily Value:** Vitamin A 60%;
Vitamin C 70%; Calcium 8%; Iron 20% ❧ **Exchanges:** 3 Starch, 3 Lean Meat, 3 Fat ❧ **Carbohydrate Choices:** 3

Betty Crocker quick & easy cookbook

Onion and Bacon Cheese Sandwiches

Prep Time **25 Minutes**
Start to Finish **25 Minutes**

4 slices bacon, cut into 1/2-inch pieces

1 medium onion, thinly sliced

8 slices (3/4 oz each) Cheddar cheese

8 slices Vienna bread, 1/2 inch thick

1 In 12-inch nonstick skillet, cook bacon over medium heat about 4 minutes, stirring occasionally, until almost cooked.

2 Add onion to skillet. Cook 2 to 3 minutes, turning occasionally, until tender. Remove bacon and onion from skillet. Reserve 1 tablespoon drippings in skillet.

3 To make each sandwich, layer cheese, bacon and onion between 2 bread slices. Place 2 sandwiches in drippings in skillet. Cover; cook over medium-low heat 3 to 5 minutes, turning once, until bread is crisp and golden brown and cheese is melted. Repeat with remaining sandwiches.

4 sandwiches

Make it a Meal

Yum, don't these sandwiches sound good? Throw your favorite frozen French fry product into the oven to serve with the sandwiches, or how about kettle-cooked potato chips? For a great no-brainer French fry dip that's a notch up from ketchup and barbecue sauce, try Cheddar-flavored sour cream or onion-and chive-flavored sour cream.

1 Sandwich: Calories 350 (Calories from Fat 170); Total Fat 19g (Saturated Fat 10g; Trans Fat 0.5g); Cholesterol 55mg; Sodium 730mg; Total Carbohydrate 27g (Dietary Fiber 2g; Sugars 2g); Protein 18g ☞ **% Daily Value:** Vitamin A 8%; Vitamin C 0%; Calcium 25%; Iron 10% ☞ **Exchanges:** 2 Starch, 1 1/2 High-Fat Meat, 1 Fat ☞ **Carbohydrate Choices:** 2

Grilled Fish Tacos

1 lb sea bass, red snapper, halibut or other firm white fish fillets

1 tablespoon olive or vegetable oil

1 teaspoon ground cumin or chili powder

1/2 teaspoon salt

1/4 teaspoon pepper

8 corn tortillas (6 inch)

1/4 cup sour cream

Toppers (shredded lettuce, chopped avocado, chopped tomatoes, chopped onion and chopped fresh cilantro), if desired

1/2 cup salsa

1 Brush grill rack with vegetable oil. Heat gas or charcoal grill.

2 Brush fish with oil; sprinkle with cumin, salt and pepper. Place fish on grill. Cover grill; cook over medium heat 5 to 7 minutes, turning once, until fish flakes easily with fork. Cut fish into 8 serving pieces.

3 Heat tortillas as directed on package. Spread sour cream on tortillas. Add fish, toppers and salsa.

8 tacos

Speed it Up

Put away the knife for those topper suggestions. Instead, pick up a layered Mexican dip from the deli case—a generous "plop" of that would taste great! Or buy preshredded lettuce, guacamole and frozen chopped onions—so you just have to chop the tomatoes.

1 Taco: Calories 160 (Calories from Fat 50); Total Fat 6g (Saturated Fat 2g; Trans Fat 0g); Cholesterol 35mg; Sodium 290mg; Total Carbohydrate 13g (Dietary Fiber 2g; Sugars 1g); Protein 13g ✎ **% Daily Value:** Vitamin A 4%; Vitamin C 2%; Calcium 8%; Iron 8% ✎ **Exchanges:** 1 Starch, 1 1/2 Very Lean Meat, 1 Fat ✎ **Carbohydrate Choices:** 1

Betty Crocker quick & easy cookbook

Grilled Portabella and Bell Pepper Sandwiches

6 fresh medium portabella mushroom caps

1 large bell pepper, cut into 1/4-inch slices

1 large red onion, sliced

1 tablespoon olive or vegetable oil

1/2 teaspoon seasoned salt

1 round focaccia bread (8 or 9 inch)

1/4 cup mayonnaise or salad dressing

1/4 cup basil pesto

4 leaf lettuce leaves

1 Heat gas or charcoal grill. Brush mushrooms, bell pepper and onion with oil. Sprinkle with seasoned salt. Place vegetables in grill basket (grill "wok").

2 Place grill basket on grill. Cover grill; cook over medium heat 10 to 12 minutes, shaking grill basket occasionally to turn vegetables, until bell pepper and onion are crisp-tender and mushrooms are just tender.

3 Cut bread horizontally in half. In small bowl, mix mayonnaise and pesto; spread over cut sides of bread. Layer lettuce and grilled vegetables on bottom half of bread. Add top of bread. Cut into 6 wedges.

6 sandwiches

Instant
Success!

It's easy to clean mushrooms just before using by wiping them off with a damp paper towel. If you find that the mushrooms are very watery after cooking, pat them dry before making the sandwiches.

1 Sandwich: Calories 350 (Calories from Fat 190); Total Fat 22g (Saturated Fat 4.5g; Trans Fat 0g); Cholesterol 10mg; Sodium 470mg; Total Carbohydrate 28g (Dietary Fiber 2g; Sugars 4g); Protein 10g ✴ **% Daily Value:** Vitamin A 4%; Vitamin C 20%; Calcium 15%; Iron 10% ✴ **Exchanges:** 1 1/2 Starch, 1 Vegetable, 1/2 High-Fat Meat, 3 1/2 Fat ✴ Carbohydrate Choices: 2

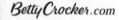

Salsa-Rice Burritos

1 1/2 cups salsa

1 1/2 teaspoons chili powder

1 cup uncooked instant rice

1 can (15 oz) black beans, drained, rinsed

1 can (11 oz) whole kernel corn with red
    and green peppers, undrained

1 1/2 cups shredded Cheddar cheese
    (6 oz)

8 flour tortillas (8 inch)

Additional salsa, if desired

1 In 10-inch skillet, heat 1 1/2 cups salsa and the chili powder to boiling. Stir in rice; remove from heat. Cover; let stand 5 minutes.

2 Stir beans, corn and cheese into rice mixture.

3 Onto center of each tortilla, spoon about 1/2 cup rice mixture. Roll tortillas around filling; tuck ends under. Serve with additional salsa.

8 burritos

Instant
Success!

If you're a meat lover and have a few extra minutes, cook up some chorizo or ground beef and stir it into the rice mixture in step 2. Some brands of chorizo come in heat-and-serve links—even easier!

1 Burrito: Calories 390 (Calories from Fat 100); Total Fat 11g (Saturated Fat 5g; Trans Fat 0.5g); Cholesterol 20mg; Sodium 680mg; Total Carbohydrate 58g (Dietary Fiber 6g; Sugars 5g); Protein 16g ❧ **% Daily Value:** Vitamin A 15%; Vitamin C 8%; Calcium 20%; Iron 20% ❧ **Exchanges:** 4 Starch, 1/2 Very Lean Meat, 1 1/2 Fat ❧ **Carbohydrate Choices:** 4

breakfast for dinner

Instant "Evening" Breakfast

"Breakfasts for dinner" can be both simple and hearty at the same time. Check out these easy and fun ideas!

1 **Egg- and Sausage-Stuffed Muffins:** Top the bottom half of a toasted English muffin with a hot cooked brown-and-serve sausage patty and a fried egg or scrambled eggs. Add a slice of American cheese if you want, too! Top with remaining muffin half.

2 **Egg Tacos:** Fill taco shells with scrambled eggs. Sprinkle with shredded cheese, purchased guacamole, salsa, sour cream and sliced ripe olives.

3 **Ham and Scrambled Egg Pockets:** Fill pita breads halves with scrambled eggs that have been cooked with chopped deli ham; sprinkle with shredded cheese.

4 **Peanut Butter–Banana Pancakes:** Heat maple-flavored syrup and peanut butter until mixture is hot and smooth (if too thick, add additional syrup). Top pancakes with sliced bananas, and serve with peanut butter–syrup mixture.

5 Merry Cherry-Chip Pancakes: Stir cherry-flavored dried cranberries and miniature semisweet chocolate chips into pancake batter. Serve with your favorite syrup and whipped topping.

6 Mexican Pancake Roll-Ups: Roll a pancake around a cooked sausage link; serve with warmed salsa or cheese dip.

7 Bacon and Swiss Waffles: Stir crumbled cooked bacon and shredded Swiss cheese into waffle batter; serve cooked waffles with melted process cheese.

8 Waffle and Fruit Bar: Serve waffles with several flavors of canned fruit pie filling and whipped topping.

9 Easy Cream Cheese–Stuffed French Toast: Before making your favorite recipe, cut a small pocket in the side of 1- to 1 1/2-inch-thick slices of French bread. Fill each slice with 1 tablespoon of your favorite fruit-flavored tub cream cheese, and cook as usual. Serve with strawberry, blueberry or maple syrup.

10 Sausage Gravy and Biscuits: Heat frozen or ready-to-eat biscuits from the bakery section of the supermarket until hot; serve with sausage gravy made from a packet mix.

This icon means: 20 minutes or less

Potato, Bacon and Egg Scramble

5 slices bacon

1 lb small red potatoes (6 or 7), cubed

6 eggs

1/3 cup milk

1/4 teaspoon salt

1/8 teaspoon pepper

2 tablespoons butter or margarine

4 medium green onions, sliced (1/4 cup)

1 In 10-inch skillet, cook bacon over medium heat 8 to 10 minutes, turning occasionally, until crisp and brown. Remove from skillet; drain on paper towels. Crumble bacon.

2 Meanwhile, in 2-quart saucepan, heat 1 inch water to boiling. Add potatoes. Cover; heat to boiling. Reduce heat to medium-low. Cook covered 6 to 8 minutes or until potatoes are tender; drain. In medium bowl, beat eggs, milk, salt and pepper with fork or wire whisk until well mixed; set aside.

3 In 10-inch skillet, melt butter over medium-high heat. Cook potatoes in butter 3 to 5 minutes, turning potatoes occasionally, until light brown. Stir in onions. Cook 1 minute, stirring constantly.

4 Pour egg mixture into skillet. As mixture begins to set at bottom and side, gently lift cooked portions with metal spatula so that thin, uncooked portion can flow to bottom. Avoid constant stirring. Cook 3 to 4 minutes or until eggs are thickened throughout but still moist. Sprinkle with crumbled bacon.

5 servings

Speed it Up

We're lucky to have so many really high-quality, great-tasting convenience foods available. If you don't have time to cube potatoes, use purchased refrigerated cubed potatoes instead.

1 Serving: Calories 260 (Calories from Fat 130); Total Fat 15g (Saturated Fat 6g; Trans Fat 0g); Cholesterol 275mg; Sodium 420mg; Total Carbohydrate 18g (Dietary Fiber 2g; Sugars 3g); Protein 13g ❧ **% Daily Value:** Vitamin A 10%; Vitamin C 10%; Calcium 8%; Iron 15% ❧ **Exchanges:** 1 Starch, 1 1/2 Medium-Fat Meat, 1 1/2 Fat ❧ **Carbohydrate Choices:** 1

Scrambled Eggs with Havarti and Wine

8 eggs

1/4 cup dry white wine or nonalcoholic wine

1/4 teaspoon salt

1/4 teaspoon pepper

2 tablespoons chopped fresh parsley

2 medium green onions, sliced (2 tablespoons)

2 tablespoons butter or margarine

4 oz Havarti cheese with dill weed, cut into 1/2-inch cubes

Additional chopped fresh parsley or dill weed, if desired

1 In medium bowl, beat eggs, wine, salt, pepper, 2 tablespoons parsley and the onions thoroughly with fork or wire whisk until well mixed.

2 In 10-inch nonstick skillet, heat butter over medium heat just until butter begins to sizzle. Pour egg mixture into skillet. Sprinkle cheese evenly over eggs.

3 As mixture begins to set at bottom and side, gently lift cooked portions with spatula so that thin, uncooked portion can flow to bottom. Avoid constant stirring. Cook 3 to 4 minutes or until eggs are thickened throughout but still moist. Garnish with additional parsley.

4 servings

Make it a Meal

When this recipe made a showing in our test kitchens, people raved. It's luscious, creamy and sophisticated—perfect for a special brunch as well as a light, elegant dinner. Serve the eggs with hash browns and brown-and-serve sausage links or bacon and some warmed scones or muffins.

1 Serving: Calories 320 (Calories from Fat 240); Total Fat 27g (Saturated Fat 14g; Trans Fat 0.5g); Cholesterol 470mg; Sodium 530mg; Total Carbohydrate 2g (Dietary Fiber 0g; Sugars 2g); Protein 19g ✷ **% Daily Value:** Vitamin A 25%; Vitamin C 2%; Calcium 20%; Iron 8% ✷ **Exchanges:** 2 1/2 Medium-Fat Meat, 3 Fat ✷ **Carbohydrate Choices:** 0

breakfast **for dinner**

Country Eggs in Tortilla Cups

4 flour tortillas (6 inch)

Cooking spray

4 eggs

1/4 cup milk

1/4 teaspoon salt

1 tablespoon butter or margarine

3 cups frozen shredded hash brown potatoes (from 32-oz bag)

1/4 cup chopped green bell pepper

1/4 cup shredded Cheddar cheese (1 oz)

Salsa, if desired

Sour cream, if desired

1 Heat oven to 400°F. Turn 4 (6-ounce) custard cups upside down onto cookie sheet. To make the tortillas more pliable, warm them as directed on the package. Spray both sides of each tortilla lightly with cooking spray. Place tortilla over each cup, gently pressing edges toward cup. Bake 8 to 10 minutes or until light golden brown. In small bowl, beat eggs, milk and salt with fork or wire whisk until well mixed; set aside.

2 Meanwhile, melt butter in 10-inch nonstick skillet over medium-high heat. Cook potatoes and bell pepper in skillet for 6 to 8 minutes, stirring occasionally, until potatoes are light golden brown; reduce heat to medium. Push potatoes to one side of skillet; carefully pour eggs into open side of skillet. Cook about 3 minutes, stirring occasionally, until eggs are almost set; sprinkle with cheese and cover 1 minute or until cheese melts.

3 Remove tortillas from cups; place upright on serving plates. Spoon 1/4 each of the potatoes and eggs into each tortilla cup. Serve with salsa and sour cream.

4 servings

Speed it Up

Look for ready-to-eat fried tortilla "bowls" in your supermarket. Or copy the new restaurant style of tortilla bowls, which is simply to fit fresh tortillas into bowls—no frying or baking! Serve with fresh fruit or a green salad.

1 Serving: Calories 350 (Calories from Fat 140); Total Fat 16g (Saturated Fat 8g, Trans Fat 0.5g); Cholesterol 190mg; Sodium 480mg; Total Carbohydrate 36g (Dietary Fiber 3g, Sugars 3g); Protein 15g ✒ **% Daily Value:** Vitamin A 10%; Vitamin C 15%; Calcium 20%; Iron 10% ✒ **Exchanges:** 2 1/2 Starch, 1 Medium-Fat Meat, 2 Fat ✒ **Carbohydrate Choices:** 2 1/2

Prep Time **20 Minutes**
Start to Finish **20 Minutes**

Bacon and Tomato Frittata

8 eggs

1/4 teaspoon salt-free garlic-and-herb
    seasoning

1/4 teaspoon salt

2 teaspoons vegetable oil

4 medium green onions, sliced
    (1/4 cup)

2 large plum (Roma) tomatoes, sliced

1/2 cup shredded sharp Cheddar
    cheese (2 oz)

2 tablespoons real bacon pieces
    (from 2.8-oz package)

2 tablespoons sour cream

1 In medium bowl, beat eggs, garlic-and-herb seasoning and salt with fork or wire whisk until well blended; set aside.

2 In 10-inch nonstick ovenproof skillet, heat oil over medium heat. Add onions; cook and stir 1 minute. Reduce heat to medium-low. Pour in egg mixture. Cook 6 to 9 minutes, gently lifting edges of cooked portions with metal spatula so that uncooked egg mixture can flow to bottom of skillet, until set.

3 Set oven control to broil. Top frittata with tomatoes, cheese and bacon. Broil with top 4 inches from heat 1 to 2 minutes or until cheese is melted. Top each serving with sour cream.

4 servings

Instant
Success!

If you don't have an ovenproof skillet, just wrap the skillet handle in a double layer of heavy-duty foil. Look for ready-to-use bacon pieces near the salad dressings in the store. They're shelf stable until opened, then they need to go in the fridge.

1 Serving: Calories 260 (Calories from Fat 180); Total Fat 20g (Saturated Fat 8g; Trans Fat 0g); Cholesterol 450mg; Sodium 470mg; Total Carbohydrate 3g (Dietary Fiber 0g; Sugars 3g); Protein 18g ✎ **% Daily Value:** Vitamin A 20%; Vitamin C 4%; Calcium 15%; Iron 8% ✎ **Exchanges:** 2 1/2 Medium-Fat Meat, 1 1/2 Fat ✎ **Carbohydrate Choices:** 0

Veggie Cream Cheese Omelets

Prep Time **20 Minutes**
Start to Finish **20 Minutes**

8 eggs

1/4 teaspoon salt

1/8 teaspoon pepper

2 tablespoons butter or margarine

1 cup 1-inch pieces fresh asparagus

1/2 red bell pepper, cut into thin slivers

1/2 cup garden vegetable cream cheese spread (from 8-oz container)

2 tablespoons chopped fresh chives

1 In medium bowl, beat eggs, salt and pepper with fork or wire whisk until well blended; set aside. In 8-inch nonstick omelet pan or skillet, heat 2 teaspoons of the butter over medium heat. Cook asparagus and bell pepper in butter 3 to 4 minutes, stirring frequently, until crisp-tender; remove from pan.

2 Add 2 teaspoons of the butter to pan. Increase heat to medium-high. Pour half of the egg mixture (scant 1 cup) into pan. As mixture begins to set at bottom and side, gently lift cooked portions with spatula so that thin, uncooked portion can flow to bottom. Avoid constant stirring. Cook 3 to 4 minutes or until eggs are thickened throughout but still moist.

3 Spoon 1/4 cup of the cream cheese in dollops evenly over omelet; top with half of the asparagus and bell pepper. Tilt skillet and slip pancake turner under omelet to loosen. Remove from heat. Fold omelet in half; remove omelet from skillet. Repeat with remaining ingredients. To serve, cut each omelet crosswise in half; sprinkle with chives.

4 servings

Make it a Meal

Toast up some English muffins or crumpets, butter them and offer some jelly and preserves, and you're good to go!

1 Serving: Calories 300 (Calories from Fat 230); Total Fat 25g (Saturated Fat 12g; Trans Fat 0.5g); Cholesterol 465mg; Sodium 520mg; Total Carbohydrate 4g (Dietary Fiber 0g; Sugars 3g); Protein 16g ⁓ **% Daily Value:** Vitamin A 40%; Vitamin C 30%; Calcium 8%; Iron 10% ⁓ **Exchanges:** 2 1/2 Medium-Fat Meat, 2 1/2 Fat ⁓ **Carbohydrate Choices:** 0

Breakfast Burritos

8 eggs

1/4 cup water

1 tablespoon butter or margarine

1 cup refried beans

1/2 cup chunky-style salsa

4 flour tortillas (10 inch)

1 cup shredded Cheddar cheese (4 oz)

Sour cream, if desired

Chopped fresh cilantro, if desired

1 In medium bowl, beat eggs and water with fork or wire whisk until well mixed.

2 In 12-inch nonstick skillet, melt butter over medium heat. Pour egg mixture into skillet. As mixture begins to set at bottom and side, gently lift cooked portions with metal spatula so that uncooked portion can flow to bottom. Cook 4 to 5 minutes or until eggs are thickened throughout but still moist; remove from heat and keep warm.

3 Spread refried beans and salsa on tortillas to within 1/2 inch of edge. Sprinkle with cheese. Place on microwavable plate; microwave each burrito uncovered on High 45 to 60 seconds or until tortilla and beans are very warm and cheese is starting to melt.

4 Cut eggs into strips, using plastic pancake turner. Divide strips evenly on centers of tortillas. Fold top and bottom ends of each tortilla about 1 inch over filling; fold right and left sides over folded ends, overlapping. Serve with sour cream and cilantro.

4 servings

Instant
Success!

Despite their name, refried beans don't have to be fried in oil or loaded with fat to be high in flavor. Canned refried beans come in regular and fat-free versions.

1 Serving: Calories 580 (Calories from Fat 260); Total Fat 28g (Saturated Fat 13g; Trans Fat 1g); Cholesterol 465mg; Sodium 970mg; Total Carbohydrate 50g (Dietary Fiber 5g; Sugars 3g); Protein 29g ✌ **% Daily Value:** Vitamin A 25%; Vitamin C 6%; Calcium 30%; Iron 25% ✌ **Exchanges:** 3 Starch, 1/2 Other Carbohydrate, 3 Medium-Fat Meat, 2 Fat ✌ **Carbohydrate Choices:** 3

Betty Crocker quick & easy cookbook

Ham and Swiss Pizza

Prep Time **15 Minutes**
Start to Finish **25 Minutes**

6 eggs, beaten

1 package (10 oz) prebaked thin Italian pizza crust (12 inch)

1/4 cup mayonnaise or salad dressing

2 tablespoons Dijon mustard

1/2 cup diced cooked ham

4 medium green onions, sliced (1/4 cup)

1/4 cup chopped red bell pepper

1 cup shredded Swiss cheese (4 oz)

1 Heat oven to 400°F. Spray 10-inch skillet with cooking spray; heat over medium heat.

2 Pour eggs into skillet. As eggs begin to set at bottom and side, gently lift cooked portions with metal spatula so that thin, uncooked portion can flow to bottom. Avoid constant stirring. Cook 3 to 4 minutes or until eggs are thickened throughout but still moist.

3 Place pizza crust on ungreased cookie sheet. In small bowl, mix mayonnaise and mustard; spread evenly over crust. Top with eggs, ham, onions, bell pepper and cheese. Bake about 10 minutes or until cheese is melted.

6 servings

Instant
Success!

Go urban chic with this Italian version—use prosciutto instead of ham and half mozzarella, half Parmesan or Asiago for the Swiss cheese.

1 Serving: Calories 370 (Calories from Fat 200); Total Fat 22g (Saturated Fat 8g; Trans Fat 0g); Cholesterol 245mg; Sodium 690mg; Total Carbohydrate 24g (Dietary Fiber 1g; Sugars 2g); Protein 19g ✖ **% Daily Value:** Vitamin A 15%; Vitamin C 10%; Calcium 20%; Iron 15% ✖ **Exchanges:** 1 1/2 Starch, 2 Medium-Fat Meat, 2 1/2 Fat ✖ **Carbohydrate Choices:** 1 1/2

Prep Time **20 Minutes**
Start to Finish **20 Minutes**

Monte Cristo Stuffed French Toast with Strawberry Syrup

12 slices French bread, 1/2 inch thick

1/4 lb shaved or very thinly sliced cooked ham

3 slices (3/4 oz each) Gruyère or Swiss cheese, cut in half

3 eggs

1/2 cup milk

2 tablespoons granulated sugar

1 tablespoon butter or margarine

Powdered sugar, if desired

3/4 cup strawberry syrup

1 Top 6 slices of the bread evenly with ham and cheese, folding to fit. Top with remaining bread slices.

2 In small bowl, beat eggs, milk and granulated sugar with fork or wire whisk until well mixed; pour into shallow bowl.

3 In 12-inch nonstick skillet, heat butter over medium-low heat. Dip each side of each sandwich in egg mixture, allowing time for bread to soak up mixture. Add sandwiches to skillet. Cover; cook 2 to 3 minutes on each side or until golden brown. Sprinkle with powdered sugar. Serve with syrup.

3 servings (2 sandwiches and 1/4 cup syrup each)

Instant Success!

Croque monsieur, or Monte Cristo sandwiches, are making a comeback! Traditionally a French-style grilled ham and cheese sandwich that has been dipped into a beaten egg mixture and fried in butter, this version becomes a rich and sensational French toast. Mix equal amounts of strawberry syrup and sour cream for a different topping flavor.

1 Serving: Calories 850 (Calories from Fat 200); Total Fat 22g (Saturated Fat 10g; Trans Fat 1g); Cholesterol 265mg; Sodium 1360mg; Total Carbohydrate 132g (Dietary Fiber 3g; Sugars 42g); Protein 31g ✎ **% Daily Value:** Vitamin A 15%; Vitamin C 0%; Calcium 35%; Iron 25% ✎ **Exchanges:** 6 Starch, 3 Other Carbohydrate, 2 Medium-Fat Meat, 1 Fat ✎ **Carbohydrate Choices:** 9

Prep Time **20 Minutes**
Start to Finish **20 Minutes**

Cream Cheese and Jam Stuffed French Toast

12 slices French bread, 1/2 inch thick

6 tablespoons cream cheese, softened

1/4 cup jam or preserves (any flavor)

3 eggs

1/2 cup milk

2 tablespoons granulated sugar

Powdered sugar, if desired

Fruit-flavored or maple-flavored syrup,
   if desired

1 Spread one side of 6 bread slices each with 1 tablespoon of the cream cheese. Spread one side of remaining bread slices with 2 teaspoons of the jam. Place 1 slice of each together to make 6 sandwiches.

2 In small bowl, beat eggs, milk and granulated sugar with fork or wire whisk until well mixed; pour into shallow bowl.

3 Spray griddle or skillet with cooking spray; heat griddle to 325°F or heat skillet over medium-low heat. Dip each side of sandwich into egg mixture. Cook sandwiches 2 to 3 minutes on each side or until golden brown. Transfer to plate; sprinkle lightly with powdered sugar. Serve with syrup.

6 servings

Speed it Up

An extremely easy alternative to stuffing the bread slices is to mix together the cream cheese and jam and spoon it on top of the hot French toast before smothering it with syrup.

1 Serving: Calories 320 (Calories from Fat 90); Total Fat 10g (Saturated Fat 5g; Trans Fat 0.5g); Cholesterol 125mg; Sodium 460mg; Total Carbohydrate 47g (Dietary Fiber 2g; Sugars 13g); Protein 11g ✽ **% Daily Value:** Vitamin A 8%; Vitamin C 0%; Calcium 10%; Iron 15% ✽ **Exchanges:** 2 Starch, 1 Other Carbohydrate, 1/2 Medium-Fat Meat, 1 1/2 Fat ✽ **Carbohydrate Choices:** 3

Prep Time **15 Minutes**
Start to Finish **15 Minutes**

Pancake and Sausage Stacks

1 package (7 oz) frozen brown-and-serve pork sausage patties (8 patties)

2 medium apples, chopped (2 cups)

1 cup maple-flavored syrup

1/2 teaspoon ground cinnamon

8 packaged frozen pancakes

1 In 12-inch nonstick skillet, mix all ingredients except pancakes. Heat to boiling; reduce heat to medium. Cook about 5 minutes, stirring occasionally, until apples are tender.

2 Meanwhile, prepare pancakes as directed on package.

3 For each serving, place 2 sausage patties on 1 pancake; spoon apple mixture over sausage. Top with additional pancake and apple mixture.

4 servings

Instant **Success!**

Want to go vegetarian? Substitute heated frozen soy-protein breakfast sausage patties for the real deal. Fry up some refrigerated potato slices with chopped green onions for a side dish.

1 Serving: Calories 660 (Calories from Fat 180); Total Fat 20g (Saturated Fat 6g; Trans Fat 0.5g); Cholesterol 45mg; Sodium 890mg; Total Carbohydrate 107g (Dietary Fiber 3g; Sugars 39g); Protein 12g ✼ **% Daily Value:** Vitamin A 4%; Vitamin C 2%; Calcium 15%; Iron 20% ✼ **Exchanges:** 2 Starch, 1/2 Fruit, 4 1/2 Other Carbohydrate, 1 High-Fat Meat, 2 Fat ✼ **Carbohydrate Choices:** 7

Betty Crocker quick & easy cookbook

Ham and Apple Pancakes

1 can (21 oz) apple pie filling

2 cups Original Bisquick mix

1 cup milk

2 eggs

3/4 cup diced cooked ham

1/2 cup shredded Cheddar cheese (2 oz)

2 medium green onions, sliced (2 tablespoons), if desired

Ground cinnamon, if desired

1 In 1-quart saucepan, heat pie filling over low heat, stirring occasionally, until hot; keep warm.

2 Meanwhile, spray griddle or skillet with cooking spray. Heat griddle to 375°F or heat skillet over medium-low heat. In large bowl, beat Bisquick mix, milk and eggs with wire whisk or egg beater until smooth. Fold in ham, cheese and onions.

3 Pour batter by 1/4 cupfuls onto hot griddle. Cook until edges are dry. Turn; cook other sides until golden brown. Serve with warm pie filling; sprinkle with cinnamon.

4 servings (3 pancakes and 1/2 cup filling each)

Instant
Success!

If you're feeling just a tad adventurous, consider livening up the pancakes by adding 1 tablespoon Dijon mustard to the batter in step 2.

1 Serving: Calories 550 (Calories from Fat 170); Total Fat 19g (Saturated Fat 7g; Trans Fat 1.5g); Cholesterol 140mg; Sodium 1380mg; Total Carbohydrate 75g (Dietary Fiber 3g; Sugars 38g); Protein 19g ✷ **% Daily Value:** Vitamin A 8%; Vitamin C 0%; Calcium 25%; Iron 15% ✷ **Exchanges:** 2 1/2 Starch, 2 1/2 Other Carbohydrate, 1 1/2 Medium-Fat Meat, 2 Fat ✷ **Carbohydrate Choices:** 5

Cheesy Pear Oven Pancake

1 cup all-purpose flour

1 cup milk

1/4 teaspoon salt

4 eggs

1 tablespoon butter or margarine

2 medium unpeeled pears, thinly sliced
(2 cups)

2 tablespoons chopped fresh or 2 teaspoons
freeze-dried chives

2 tablespoons sugar

3/4 cup shredded Cheddar cheese (3 oz)

1 Heat oven to 450°F. Spray 13 × 9-inch (3-quart) glass baking dish with cooking spray. In medium bowl, beat flour, milk, salt and eggs with wire whisk until smooth. Pour into baking dish. Bake 15 to 18 minutes or until puffy and golden brown.

2 Meanwhile, in 10-inch nonstick skillet, melt butter over medium-high heat. Cook pears and chives in butter about 5 minutes, stirring frequently, until pears are slightly softened. Stir in sugar.

3 Spoon pear mixture onto pancake. Sprinkle with cheese. Bake about 1 minute or until cheese is melted.

4 servings

1 Serving: Calories 410 (Calories from Fat 150); Total Fat 17g (Saturated Fat 9g; Trans Fat 0g); Cholesterol 245mg; Sodium 390mg; Total Carbohydrate 47g (Dietary Fiber 4g; Sugars 19g); Protein 17g ✒ **% Daily Value:** Vitamin A 15%; Vitamin C 4%; Calcium 20%; Iron 15% ✒ **Exchanges:** 2 Starch, 1/2 Fruit, 1/2 Other Carbohydrate, 1 1/2 Medium-Fat Meat, 1 1/2 Fat ✒ **Carbohydrate Choices:** 3

helpful nutrition and cooking information

Nutrition Guidelines

We provide nutrition information for each recipe that includes calories, fat, cholesterol, sodium, carbohydrate, fiber and protein. Individual food choices can be based on this information.

Recommended intake for a daily diet of 2,000 calories as set by the Food and Drug Administration

Total Fat	Less than 65g
Saturated Fat	Less than 20g
Cholesterol	Less than 300mg
Sodium	Less than 2,400mg
Total Carbohydrate	300g
Dietary Fiber	25g

Criteria Used for Calculating Nutrition Information

- The first ingredient was used wherever a choice is given (such as 1/3 cup sour cream or plain yogurt).

- The first ingredient amount was used wherever a range is given (such as 3- to 3 1/2–pound cut-up broiler-fryer chicken).

- The first serving number was used wherever a range is given (such as 4 to 6 servings).

- "If desired" ingredients and recipe variations were not included (such as sprinkle with brown sugar, if desired).

- Only the amount of a marinade or frying oil that is estimated to be absorbed by the food during preparation or cooking was calculated.

Ingredients Used in Recipe Testing and Nutrition Calculations

- Ingredients used for testing represent those that the majority of consumers use in their homes: large eggs, 2% milk, 80%-lean ground beef, canned ready-to-use chicken broth and vegetable oil spread containing not less than 65 percent fat.

- Fat-free, low-fat or low-sodium products were not used, unless otherwise indicated.

- Solid vegetable shortening (not butter, margarine, nonstick cooking sprays or vegetable oil spread as they can cause sticking problems) was used to grease pans, unless otherwise indicated.

Equipment Used in Recipe Testing

We use equipment for testing that the majority of consumers use in their homes. If a specific piece of equipment (such as a wire whisk) is necessary for recipe success, it is listed in the recipe.

- Cookware and bakeware without nonstick coatings were used, unless otherwise indicated.

- No dark-colored, black or insulated bakeware was used.

- When a pan is specified in a recipe, a metal pan was used; a baking dish or pie plate means ovenproof glass was used.

- An electric hand mixer was used for mixing only when mixer speeds are specified in the recipe directions. When a mixer speed is not given, a spoon or fork was used.

Cooking Terms Glossary

BEAT: Mix ingredients vigorously with spoon, fork, wire whisk, hand beater or electric mixer until smooth and uniform.

BOIL: Heat liquid until bubbles rise continuously and break on the surface and steam is given off. For rolling boil, the bubbles form rapidly.

CHOP: Cut into coarse or fine irregular pieces with a knife, food chopper, blender or food processor.

CUBE: Cut into squares 1/2 inch or larger.

DICE: Cut into squares smaller than 1/2 inch.

GRATE: Cut into tiny particles using small rough holes of grater (citrus peel or chocolate).

GREASE: Rub the inside surface of a pan with shortening, using pastry brush, piece of waxed paper or paper towel, to prevent food from sticking during baking (as for some casseroles).

JULIENNE: Cut into thin, matchlike strips, using knife or food processor (vegetables, fruits, meats).

MIX: Combine ingredients in any way that distributes them evenly.

SAUTÉ: Cook foods in hot oil or margarine over medium-high heat with frequent tossing and turning motion.

SHRED: Cut into long thin pieces by rubbing food across the holes of a shredder, as for cheese, or by using a knife to slice very thinly, as for cabbage.

SIMMER: Cook in liquid just below the boiling point on top of the stove; usually after reducing heat from a boil. Bubbles will rise slowly and break just below the surface.

STIR: Mix ingredients until uniform consistency. Stir once in a while for stirring occasionally, often for stirring frequently and continuously for stirring constantly.

TOSS: Tumble ingredients (such as green salad) lightly with a lifting motion, usually to coat evenly or mix with another food.

metric conversion guide

VOLUME

U.S. Units	Canadian Metric	Australian Metric
1/4 teaspoon	1 mL	1 ml
1/2 teaspoon	2 mL	2 ml
1 teaspoon	5 mL	5 ml
1 tablespoon	15 mL	20 ml
1/4 cup	50 mL	60 ml
1/3 cup	75 mL	80 ml
1/2 cup	125 mL	125 ml
2/3 cup	150 mL	170 ml
3/4 cup	175 mL	190 ml
1 cup	250 mL	250 ml
1 quart	1 liter	1 liter
1 1/2 quarts	1.5 liters	1.5 liters
2 quarts	2 liters	2 liters
2 1/2 quarts	2.5 liters	2.5 liters
3 quarts	3 liters	3 liters
4 quarts	4 liters	4 liters

WEIGHT

U.S. Units	Canadian Metric	Australian Metric
1 ounce	30 grams	30 grams
2 ounces	55 grams	60 grams
3 ounces	85 grams	90 grams
4 ounces (1/4 pound)	115 grams	125 grams
8 ounces (1/2 pound)	225 grams	225 grams
16 ounces (1 pound)	455 grams	500 grams
1 pound	455 grams	1/2 kilogram

MEASUREMENTS

Inches	Centimeters
1	2.5
2	5.0
3	7.5
4	10.0
5	12.5
6	15.0
7	17.5
8	20.5
9	23.0
10	25.5
11	28.0
12	30.5
13	33.0

TEMPERATURES

Fahrenheit	Celsius
32°	0°
212°	100°
250°	120°
275°	140°
300°	150°
325°	160°
350°	180°
375°	190°
400°	200°
425°	220°
450°	230°
475°	240°
500°	260°

NOTE: The recipes in this cookbook have not been developed or tested using metric measures. When converting recipes to metric, some variations in quality may be noted.

index

Note: *Italicized* page references indicate photographs.

This icon means: 🕐 **20 minutes or less**

Complete your cookbook library
with these *Betty Crocker* titles

Betty Crocker Baking for Today
Betty Crocker Basics
Betty Crocker's Best Bread Machine Cookbook
Betty Crocker's Best Chicken Cookbook
Betty Crocker's Best of Baking
Betty Crocker's Best of Healthy and Hearty Cooking
Betty Crocker's Best-Loved Recipes
Betty Crocker's Bisquick® Cookbook
Betty Crocker Bisquick® II Cookbook
Betty Crocker Bisquick® Impossibly Easy Pies
Betty Crocker Celebrate!
Betty Crocker Christmas Cookbook
Betty Crocker's Complete Thanksgiving Cookbook
Betty Crocker's Cook Book for Boys and Girls
Betty Crocker's Cook It Quick
Betty Crocker Cookbook, 10th Edition— *The* **BIG RED** *Cookbook*®
Betty Crocker Cookbook, Bonus Edition
Betty Crocker Cookbook, Bridal Edition
Betty Crocker Cookbook for Women
Betty Crocker's Cookie Book
Betty Crocker's Cooking Basics
Betty Crocker's Cooking for Two
Betty Crocker's Cooky Book, Facsimile Edition
Betty Crocker Decorating Cakes and Cupcakes
Betty Crocker's Diabetes Cookbook
Betty Crocker Dinner Made Easy with Rotisserie Chicken
Betty Crocker Easy Everyday Vegetarian
Betty Crocker Easy Family Dinners
Betty Crocker's Easy Slow Cooker Dinners
Betty Crocker's Eat and Lose Weight
Betty Crocker's Entertaining Basics
Betty Crocker's Flavors of Home
Betty Crocker 4-Ingredient Dinners
Betty Crocker Grilling Made Easy
Betty Crocker Healthy Heart Cookbook
Betty Crocker's Healthy New Choices
Betty Crocker's Indian Home Cooking
Betty Crocker's Italian Cooking
Betty Crocker's Kids Cook!
Betty Crocker's Kitchen Library
Betty Crocker's Living with Cancer Cookbook
Betty Crocker Low-Carb Lifestyle Cookbook
Betty Crocker's Low-Fat, Low-Cholesterol Cooking Today
Betty Crocker More Slow Cooker Recipes
Betty Crocker's New Chinese Cookbook
Betty Crocker One-Dish Meals
Betty Crocker's A Passion for Pasta
Betty Crocker's Picture Cook Book, Facsimile Edition
Betty Crocker's Slow Cooker Cookbook
Betty Crocker's Ultimate Cake Mix Cookbook
Betty Crocker Why It Works
Betty Crocker Win at Weight Loss Cookbook
Cocina Betty Crocker